Editor
Sara Connolly

Managing Editor
Ina Massler Levin, M.A.

Illustrator
Renée Christine Yates

Cover Artist
Brenda DiAntonis

Art Manager
Kevin Barnes

Art Director
CJae Froshay

Imaging
James Edward Grace
Rosa C. See

Publisher
Mary D. Smith, M.S. Ed.

World History

Grades 5–8

Includes Standards & Benchmarks

Author

Wendy Conklin, M.A.

Teacher Created Resources

Teacher Created Resources, Inc.
6421 Industry Way
Westminster, CA 92683
www.teachercreated.com
ISBN: 978-1-4206-3048-0
©2005 Teacher Created Resources, Inc.
Reprinted, 2012
Made in U.S.A.

Table of Contents

Introduction

Why Study Mysteries?

What are the answers to the mysteries in world history? What happened to the Knights Templars and their treasure? Who was the Man in the Iron Mask? Did Marco Polo really travel to China? Did Shakespeare really write those great works? Did someone murder Mozart? Who was Beethoven's Immortal Beloved? What happened to the crew aboard the *Mary Celeste*? Could the sinking of the *Lusitania* have been prevented? Why did the Peking Man bones disappear and who has them today? Will we ever really know the truth to these mysteries? Probably not, and that is precisely what makes these mysteries so useful to us today.

Why should we ask questions that cannot be answered with absolute certainty? Asking these types of questions demands that students speculate, debate, gather evidence, judge, evaluate, and compare. In this process, students use higher level thinking skills. Their capacity to think critically increases with each new ambiguity. This book is designed to help students think critically. At first, these lessons might frustrate the student who always wants the one right answer. But as teachers learn to handle these frustrations and encourage students to think for themselves, students will grow to love these types of stories where there is no one right answer. In addition, these lessons enable students the opportunity to generate creative products like tabloids, newspaper headlines, campaign slogans for a candidate, written confessions, certificates of death, letters, stamps, statements, and expedition plans.

How This Book Is Organized

There are nine mysteries in this book. While the activities vary within each mystery, the layout for implementing the lessons is the same. Each mystery begins with an attention grabber. Some of these are in the form of primary sources, such as diary entries and newspaper articles, and others are eye-catching posters and simulations. Students have the opportunity to discuss these attention grabbers. Each mystery also has a graphic organizer so that students can keep track of what they are learning. Every piece of background information needed for each mystery is provided in this unit. Teachers will not need to research beyond what is provided here. If students want to look into other aspects of the mysteries, resources are available in the bibliography at the end of the unit. The activities vary within each mystery. One has students put on a trial, another allows students to work for a newspaper, and yet another instructs students to work as investigators. Each mystery allows students to become experts. They pull together pieces of information and make the final decision on the mystery while providing evidence as support for their views.

The Knights Templars and Their Treasure

Teacher Lesson Plan

Standard/Objective

❋ Develop critical sensitivities, such as empathy and skepticism, regarding attitudes, values, and behaviors of people in different historical contexts. (NCSS)

❋ Students will decide the guilt or innocence of the Knights Templars and then speculate on the whereabouts of their treasures, revealing their answers on magazine covers.

Materials

❋ copies of *Background Information* (pages 9–12); *Graphic Organizer* (page 13); *T-Chart* (page 14); *The Stone* (page 15); *More Treasure Information* (page 16); *Time Line of Events* (pages 17–18); *Tabloid News!* (page 19)

❋ overhead copy of the *Attention Grabber* (page 8)

❋ large sheets of paper

Discussion Questions

❋ Who are the Knights Templars?

❋ What are the requirements for joining the Knights Templars?

❋ What could be so mysterious about the Knights Templars?

❋ What do you think the Knights Templars name means?

The Activity: Day 1

Before students come into class, write each discussion question at the top of a large sheet of butcher paper and place the questions around the room. Ask students if they have ever heard of the Knights Templars. Write this name on the board so that students can see it. Ask students to speculate on this group of individuals by writing answers to the discussion questions posted around the room. Have students find partners and walk around the room answering the posted discussion questions. Instruct students to try and find something new to contribute to each paper. They should not copy answers already written, but they can add to other answers or make up their own unique answers. During the discussion, some students might make the connection that the word *Templars* comes from the word *temple*. If not, point that out. Then students might be able to brainstorm more ideas about their identity. When students have finished brainstorming ideas to these questions, bring them back together.

Teacher Lesson Plan *(cont.)*

The Activity: Day 1 (cont.)

Place the *Attention Grabber* (page 8) on the overhead with only the first line showing. Give students a few minutes to read it and talk with their neighbors about it. Then reveal more information line by line, stopping to talk about who they think the Knights Templars are.

Then tell students that they will use this information to create a resume for this job. Students can work with a partner or individually on this creative project. Explain that they want to make themselves look qualified for the position. If possible, show simplified examples of a resume so that students will understand that they need personal information as well as information that tells how their previous jobs make them qualified for this position. Share these resumes with the class when complete. Explain to students that they will find out more about this mysterious group on the following day.

The Activity: Day 2

Begin by reminding students of the resumes they prepared the previous day. Then distribute copies of the *Background Information* (pages 9–12) and read it aloud as a class. Stop frequently and ask questions as you read aloud to make sure that students understand this information. Have students keep the Background Information in a safe place so that they can refer back to it during the week.

Then distribute copies of the *Graphic Organizer* (page 13). Have students use the background information to help them explore all the possibilities of what happened to the Knights Templars and what happened to their treasure. Students can work with a partner as they fill out their organizers. Remind students that they will be referring back to this organizer throughout the week.

Wanted: Individuals to join the Knights Templars immediately.

These individuals should be mighty warriors and devoutly religious with impeccable morals.

Job duties include protecting pilgrims as they travel to and from the holy city of Jerusalem.

Individuals should also be willing to take an oath of poverty upon joining.

Send resumes to Jerusalem Palace addressed to Jacques de Molay.

Teacher Lesson Plan *(cont.)*

The Activity: Day 3

Begin by reminding students of the background information from the previous class. It might be helpful for them to take a quick look at their graphic organizers. Students will be looking at whether or not the Knights Templars were guilty of the charges brought against them by King Philip. Have students work with partners to fill out the *T-Chart* (page 14) listing reasons the Knights Templars were guilty and reasons they were innocent of Philip the Fair's allegations. Reasons for guilt might include their confessions to the king, their confessions to the Pope, their secret initiation rights, the fact that their freedom and wealth allowed them to do what they wanted, the idea that rumors sometimes hold a little truth, and more. Reasons that they are innocent might include that Philip was a greedy ruler who wanted their money, the confessions were coerced by torture, the Knights Templars recanted their confessions even though they knew they would die for doing so, they had no allies to support their cause because everyone was jealous, and so on.

Then have students share their T-Charts in small groups. Have each group compile a group T-Chart and present it to the class. Finally, have students revisit their graphic organizers and add any important information to them.

The Activity: Day 4

Tell students that they not only need to think about the guilt or innocence of the Knights Templars, they also need to think about what happened to their treasure.

Before class, write the first four discussion questions below at the top of large pieces of butcher paper or posterboard and post them around the room.

Then take *The Stone* (page 15) and "bury" it somewhere in the classroom. One idea is to place it under a student's desk so that students can find it easily. Once students have discovered it, distribute a copy of it to each student.

- What is mysterious about this discovery?
- What do you think this writing means?
- For what reasons do people use secret messages?
- Why would someone leave a message like this?
- Does this make you think that the message is a hoax or real?

Teacher Lesson Plan *(cont.)*

The Activity: Day 4 (cont.)

Have students work with partners and walk around the room adding answers to each of the discussion questions. Explain that they cannot copy anyone else's answers, but they can add to other answers already posted or they can write a new answer. Students will be reading what others have written as they carousel around answering each question.

Bring the class back together and tell them that you have the answer to this encrypted code. Write this message on the board: "Forty Feet Below Two Million Pounds are Buried." Then ask the remaining discussion question and have students explain their answers. For example, some might think that the code is a hoax because if it was authentic, the hiding place would no longer be a secret.

Explain to students that this stone was really found on an island in Canada back at the beginning of the 1800s. The reason why it is included in this mystery is because some think that the treasure buried there has to do with the Knights Templars.

Distribute copies of *More Treasure Information* (page 16) and *Time Line of Events* (pages 17–18). Have students read the handouts and then take out their graphic organizers and record any helpful information on them.

Answer Key

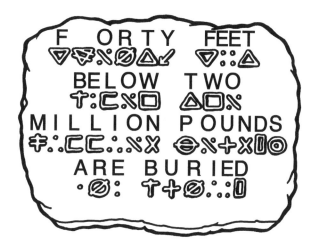

The Activity: Day 5

Begin by having students review their information on the graphic organizers. Tell them that they will be making two decisions today about the Knights Templars. First, they must decide whether or not the Templars are guilty of King Philip's accusations. Second, they must decide what happened to the Templars' treasure. Distribute copies of *Tabloid News!* (page 19) Have students create magazine covers that tell their decisions on both issues. If time permits, have students share their magazine covers with the class and discuss how each one is different.

Attention Grabber

Wanted: Individuals to join the Knights Templars immediately.

These individuals should be mighty warriors and devoutly religious with impeccable morals.

Job duties include protecting pilgrims as they travel to and from the holy city of Jerusalem.

Individuals should also be willing to take an oath of poverty upon joining.

Send resumes to Jerusalem Palace addressed to Jacques de Molay.

The Knights Templars and Their Treasure

Background Information

During the Middle Ages, knights from Europe invaded the area of the Middle East called the Holy Land. These knights were Christians and these invasions were called the Crusades. The purpose of the Crusades was to take back the Holy Land or Palestine (called Israel today) for the Christians. Muslim rulers had control of the land at that time.

In 1099, the Christians defeated Jerusalem. By 1119, a group of knights had banded together to protect the people who traveled from Europe to the Holy Land. It is believed that there were 20,000 of them at one time. The knights' duty was to protect Jerusalem and the pilgrims who traveled there. Pilgrims faced the threat of thieves and pirates along the way. By day the knights were warriors and by night they were religious monks who prayed.

Background Information *(cont.)*

The king of Jerusalem blessed them and let them stay in his palace. This king's palace was on the site where a famous king named Solomon had once built a temple a long time ago. Because they stayed on the site of the temple, the knights were called the Poor Knights of the Temple or Knights Templars. They took vows of poverty, but their poverty did not last for very long. The Knights Templars soon became very rich. In fact, they were the richest group of people in the medieval world. Their religious conduct, along with their warrior abilities, attracted the attention of many rulers throughout Europe. These rulers competed for the Templars' attention by giving them many gifts. The rulers did not make the Templars pay tax, either. The Templars' wealth began to accumulate.

Soon the Templars became the first bankers in Europe. Rulers sent money to them and the Templars issued the ruler a letter of credit which could be redeemed anywhere. In no time at all the Templars had as much power as any king or queen. By the end of the 1200s, the only person more powerful than the Templars was the Pope. It was also about this time that Jerusalem was taken back by the Muslims and all the Templars were expelled. Luckily, their money headquarters was in Paris, so financially they still seemed safe.

But resentment had been building against the Templars for quite a while. Other groups were jealous that they held so much money and power. They had secret initiation rights and others did not like the secrecy. The Templars acted as though they did not have to answer to anyone. This arrogant attitude made many people angry and they refused to help them when the Templars were in trouble. Soon accusations began flying against the Templars. Some accused the Templars of being Satan worshippers, the worst accusation possible at the time.

The main leader accusing the Templars was the powerful King of France, Philip the Fair. He tried to convince the pope to perform an investigation, but the Pope refused to listen. So Philip the Fair began his own investigation and arrested all the Templars in France. The Pope protested by saying that he alone had power over the Templars, but Philip ignored him. Under torture, many of the knights admitted to spitting on the crucifix and to other anti-Christian behavior. Some claimed that they worshipped idols in the forms of cats or other animals.

Background Information *(cont.)*

The pope did not believe the confessions of these knights. He believed that the king of France pressured them into lying. However, in 1308, 72 of these knights confessed right in front of the pope. The pope was forced to launch an official investigation throughout Europe. In some places these knights were tortured, and in other places they were simply questioned. When the knights were tortured, there were more confessions. It took years for him to complete the investigation.

After a while, the Templars who had confessed in France began retracting their confessions. They claimed their confessions were all lies. Any knight who retracted his confession was immediately placed under the authority of the state. In France, this authority was Philip the Fair. King Philip did not have any mercy on those who retracted. He had them immediately burned at the stake. The leader of the Templars, Jacques de Molay, decided he could not live with his "false" confession either. It took him four years, but he finally retracted his confession, too. He was burned at the stake in front of Notre Dame in Paris. Legend says that out of the fire, his voice was heard telling the Pope and King Philip to meet him in heaven to determine justice. Many believed he was calling down a curse on them. Both the Pope and the King were dead within a year.

The Pope had already officially disbanded the Knights Templars everywhere except for Spain and Portugal. These groups were allowed to continue but had to change their names. Everywhere else their money, possessions, and land were seized and used by rulers. Some say a greedy king who could control a weak pope wrongly accused the Templars. Others say that the Templars were conspiring to turn many people away from Christianity and the Church.

Background Information *(cont.)*

Many theories surround the Knights Templars. Was all their wealth taken or was some of it secretly hidden? Did any of the Knights Templars continue the society illegally under a different name? One legend claims that on the day of the mass arrests in France, the Templars' wealth was taken out of the country on a boat. This wealth was loaded onto a wagon and taken to the port city of La Rochelle. It was then loaded onto a Templar ship and taken to a secret location where the remaining Templars used it to set up an underground organization. One theory says that they went to Scotland with the wealth and eventually emerged as the Freemasons. Some think the remaining Templars went to Scotland and helped the Scots under Robert Bruce defeat the English under King Edward I in 1314. They say it was their warrior presence that won a decisive battle for Bruce. Freemasonry did emerge in Scotland in the 1700s, so could both of these theories tie together? There is not enough evidence to prove or disprove any of these theories.

There is a story that claims that their treasure was buried in Nova Scotia, Canada, on Oak Island. This treasure area is called the Money Pit. No one knows exactly what is buried in the Money Pit because complete excavations have not yet taken place. Some think that the Templars had famous relics from Jerusalem like the Ark of the Covenant and the Holy Grail. They claim that the Templars took these relics when they secretly excavated Solomon's temple while living in Jerusalem. The Money Pit is marked with a stone cross, a sign typical of the Templars. Whatever happened to the Templars and all their wealth will continue to remain a mystery.

Graphic Organizer

Mapping Solutions

Directions: Use this page to create a flow chart about the Knights Templars and their treasure. Your flow chart can go in many different directions. This page will help you keep track of that information in an organized way. Add as many arrows as you need to record all the information.

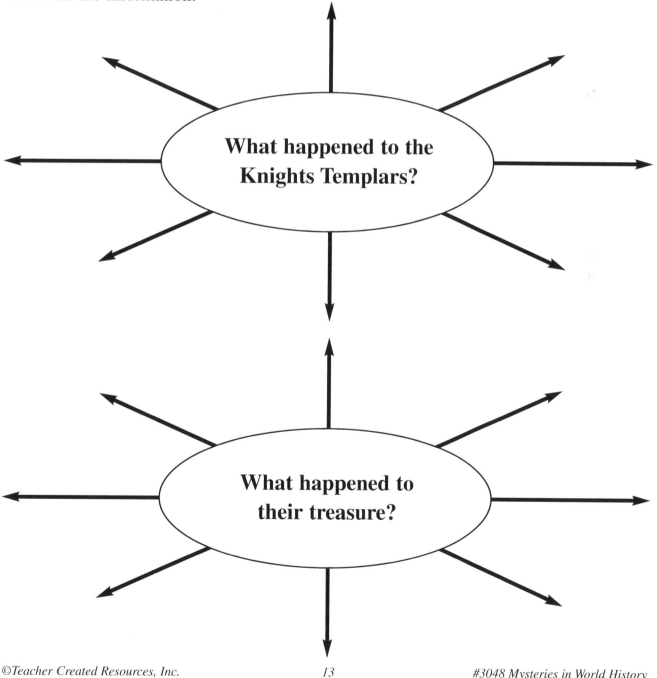

The Knights Templars and Their Treasure

T-Chart

Directions: Were the Knights Templars guilty of what Philip the Fair accused them? Why would he accuse them? If they were not guilty, then why did they confess? Think about their guilt or innocence. Then write the reasons for guilt on one side of the T-chart and the reasons for innocence on the other side of the T-chart.

The Templars Are Guilty	The Templars Are Innocent

The Stone

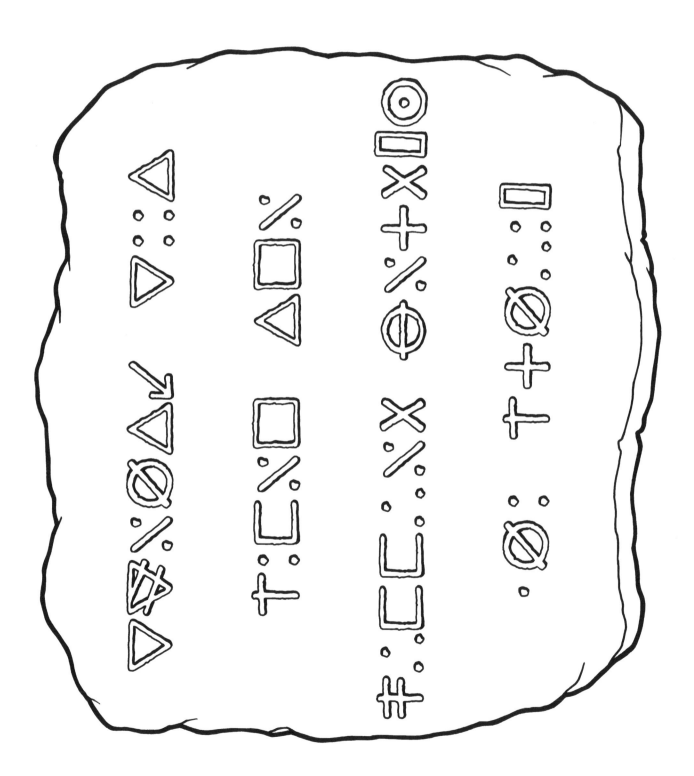

More Treasure Information

Is the Treasure at Oak Island in Nova Scotia?

A 16 year old boy named Daniel McGinnis first discovered the Money Pit in 1795. He had been fishing for the day. He docked his boat at Oak Island and walked across the land. Suddenly he saw a scarred oak tree with a hole near it. He believed it was a place of buried treasure, possibly by pirates, and that a make-shift crane caused the scarring on the tree. He returned with two friends. As they dug, they discovered they would need better tools. They left and returned almost nine years later to find the site as they had left it. This time they had financial backing and the needed tools to excavate the site. Everyone working there had a claim in the treasure, if it was found.

After digging through layers of oak logs, boards, charcoal, putty, and coconut fiber, they suddenly hit a stone at 90 feet deep. This stone had a puzzling inscription on it that has not yet been deciphered.

When they dug down deep enough and struck what they thought to be a treasure chest, the shaft flooded with water. It appeared that the hole was booby-trapped. They could not reach the treasure. For years different groups tried to reach the treasure and several men died in the process.

After many investigations and failed attempts at excavating, people are still divided on what they believe about the Oak Island treasure. Some believe the shafts and booby trap elements of the hole are not man made. They say these holes are just natural sink holes that could be found on any island. But no one can refute the evidence of the encrypted stone. Was this stone merely a hoax or was it a real clue explaining where the treasure was buried?

Time Line of Events

1795   Daniel McGinnis finds the Money Pit and digs with friends, John Smith and Anthony Vaughan, to a depth of 30 feet. It was too hard, so they gave up and went to find more help.

1803   The Onslow Company together with Daniel and his friends begins excavating the site. When they reach a depth of 90 feet they find an inscribed stone. The shaft becomes flooded as water quickly seeps into it.

1804   In hopes of reaching the pit without flooding, the Onslow Company digs next to the pit to a depth of 110 feet. Water floods that hole when they attempt to tunnel across into the Money Pit.

1849   Another company, the Truro Company, begins digging. They drilled through two casks filled with loose metal thought to be coins. Parts of a gold chain found there vanished.

1850   A waterway and fake beach are found at a cove, which is discovered to flood the pit.

1861   Several cross tunnels have weakened the pit, causing the bottom to fall out. Because of this, items that were suspected to lie at 100 feet fall farther down into the earth.

Time Line of Events *(cont.)*

1893   The cave-in pit is investigated when Fred Blair and The Oak Island Treasure Company begin their investigations.

1899   A second flood tunnel on the south shore of the island was discovered.

1936   A second inscribed stone was found.

1959   Four more lives were lost from carbon monoxide poisoning in the pit.

1965   A 70-ton digging crane is used to apply modern open pit mining methods.

1970   Triton begins digging on the island and commissioned a complete geological survey of the area. Their discoveries are never made public, but they continue digging today.

1971   Video footage shows what is believed to be two chests and a severed hand.

Tabloid News!

Directions: Create a cover for a magazine that tells your decisions about the Knights Templars. Are they guilty of King Philip's charges? Or are they innocent? Add something to your magazine cover that tells what happened to their treasure.

Did Marco Polo Really Travel to China?

Teacher Lesson Plan

Standard/Objective

* ✳ Demonstrate an understanding that different scholars may describe the same event or situation in different ways but must provide reasons or evidence for their views. (NCSS)

* ✳ Students will participate as jurors in a court case that tries Marco Polo for fraudulent behavior and then decide whether he is guilty or not guilty.

Materials

* ✳ copies of the *Attention Grabber* (pages 24); *Graphic Organizer* (page 25); *Background Information* (pages 26-28); *The Prosecution's Case* (pages 29–30); *Polo's Voyage Map* (page 31); *The Defense's Case* (pages 32–33); *Jury Vote* (page 34); *Newspaper Headlines* (page 35)

* ✳ envelopes (one for each student)

Discussion Questions

* ✳ What is a jury summons?

* ✳ Who do you think is being brought to trial?

* ✳ What do you think this case will be about?

* ✳ What qualities does an effective juror have?

* ✳ Do you think you are capable of being a good juror? Why or why not?

The Activity: Day 1

To get students excited about this lesson, make copies of the *Attention Grabber* (page 24) and place each one in an envelope. Then give each student an envelope as he or she arrives in class. Inside this envelope is a jury summons to appear at the City-State of Venice's official courtroom (which will be your classroom). Then ask the discussion questions above. This can be done in small groups or in a classroom discussion. It is important for students to know the role of a juror. Have students work in small groups to write out possible answers to the fourth question above. Let groups present their lists describing a good juror to the class.

Explain to students that this court case is set for the year 1300 A.D. The City-State of Venice is trying a man by the name of Marco Polo for fraud. Have students look up the word *fraud* in a dictionary. Distribute copies of the *Graphic Organizer* (page 25). Remind students that they should record their notes about the trial on this graphic organizer. Have students brainstorm a list of things they know about Marco Polo. This information can be added to their graphic organizers, too. Then have these small groups brainstorm reasons why the charge of fraud is being brought against him. What could he have done wrong? Share these ideas with the class.

Did Marco Polo Really Travel to China?

Teacher Lesson Plan (cont.)

The Activity: Day 1 (cont.)

Distribute copies of the *Background Information* (pages 26–28) to students and have them read it in small groups. This information gives the well-known history about Marco Polo. Much of it talks about his travels and the route that he took.

After reading the information, let students fill in the *Graphic Organizer* (page 25). This organizer will help students to keep track of the information about Marco Polo. It will be used every day of the trial.

Give students their jury instructions. They will be hearing the prosecution's case against Marco Polo first, and then they will hear the defense's case. Tell students that because they are jurors, they are not allowed to talk about this case to anyone, especially to the other jurors in this room. Remind students that jurors are not allowed to discuss the trial until both cases have rested. In addition, tell students that they are being sequestered for this trial. When a jury is sequestered, it means that they are not allowed to go home, read the paper, turn on the news, or listen to the radio. For this jury, being sequestered means that they are not allowed to read any information about this trial (on the Internet, or in books, etc.). In addition, they are not allowed to talk about it with anyone outside this classroom.

At the end of the class period, distribute the student page, *Jury Vote* (page 34). Have students write down their votes, and collect the papers from them. Make sure that students have written their names on their pages. This is a preliminary vote of what students think about Marco Polo's guilt or innocence. This vote should be kept confidential. A vote will be taken each day of the trial. Be sure to explain to students that the votes taken each day will be tallied for that day and the results will be shared daily. Explain to students that it is common for juries to take multiple votes before making a final decision.

The Activity: Day 2

Distribute *The Prosecution's Case* (pages 29–30) to the class and read it aloud. This information deals with the problems with Polo's account of his travel. Students are not allowed to ask questions. They are not allowed to discuss this information. It is only to be read.

After reading the information, let students fill in the *Graphic Organizer* (page 25) with any pertinent information they will need to remember about this trial.

Then distribute copies of *Polo's Voyage Map* (page 31). This map shows the route that Polo took on his journey. It will help students visualize Polo's journey better. Explain that the defense will present its case the next day. At the end of the class period, distribute the student page, *Jury Vote* (page 34). Allow students to vote, and then collect these papers. Each individual vote should be kept confidential, but the final outcome should be shared with the class. Remind students of the vote totals from the previous day.

Teacher Lesson Plan *(cont.)*

The Activity: Day 3

Remind students of the jury instructions. Tell students that they will be reviewing more evidence from the case today. Since the prosecution has presented their case, the defense now has a turn to do the same. Distribute *The Defense's Case* (pages 32–33). This information defends Marco Polo and the claims that he made about his travels. Simply read the information aloud, but do not allow students to talk about the case or ask any questions. Let students fill in any additional information needed on their graphic organizer. At the end of the class period, distribute the student page, *Jury Vote* (page 34) and collect these papers. Each individual vote should be kept confidential, but the vote total should be shared. Remind students of the vote totals from the day before.

The Activity: Day 4

When students come into class, remind them that after both sides have rested their case, the jurors finally get a chance to talk about the trial and find out how everyone feels. Tell students that they are to present a short (2–3 minutes) persuasive speech in front of their fellow jurors. This speech is meant to persuade the other jurors to their view. Give students a few minutes to prepare their speech. Then let students hash out the case. Everyone should have a chance to present his or her speech.

At the end of the class, take another *Jury Vote* (page 34). This will be the final vote as to whether or not Marco Polo committed fraud with his book. The majority vote from this day only will decide Polo's innocence or guilt.

Ask students to reflect on how their votes have changed as more evidence has been presented. Then ask students to reflect on how their votes changed after they talked with their fellow jurors. Although students have had a chance to talk about the trial, remind them that they are still not allowed to discuss this trial with people outside the classroom. This trial can only be talked about inside this classroom with other jurors. This lesson is not over yet!

Day 1 Vote:	Day 2 Vote:
Not Guilty	*Guilty*
Day 3 Vote:	Day 4 Vote:
Not Guilty	*Guilty*

Teacher Lesson Plan *(cont.)*

The Activity: Day 5

Even though Marco Polo's case has been tried and is decided, some of the jurors may still disagree with the verdict. Distribute *Newspaper Headlines* (page 35) to students and have them write headlines about this case. If a student feels that Marco Polo lied about his journey, the headline should reflect that. If a student feels that Marco Polo really did tell the truth, the headline should say so. Let students share these headlines with the class and then post them for all to see.

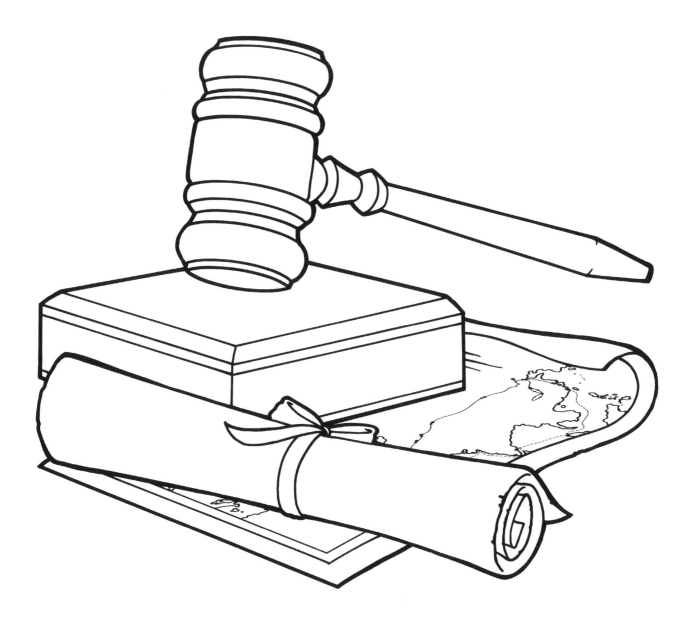

Attention Grabber

Jury Summons

Official Document

Jury Summons—Do Not Discard

You are hereby summoned to be available as a trial juror for the City-State of Venice official court.

Week of Availability	Juror Number

Return This Questionnaire within 5 Days of Receipt

Name	Birth Date
Address	
City, State	Zip Code
Phone	
Have you ever been called to serve as a juror?	
Have you or has any member of your immediate family served as a witness?	
Have you or has any member of your immediate family ever been sued?	
Are you either a close friend of or are you related to any law enforcement officer?	
Have you ever been convicted of a crime?	

Graphic Organizer

Jury Notes

Directions: Record any pertinent information about the Marco Polo case on this sheet. Keep this with you throughout the trial for reference.

Who is speaking?	His or her important point?	Do I agree? Why or Why not?

Did Marco Polo Really Travel to China?

Background Information

Marco Polo was born in 1254 into an adventurous family who lived in Venice, Italy. In 1298, he wrote a book which tells about his family and the adventures of his father and uncle. His father, Niccolo, and uncle, Maffeo, were jewel merchants and had spent all fifteen years of Marco's early life on an amazing adventure exploring the Far East. There, they had met the great Kublai Khan, son of Genghis Khan. (Khan was a title given to Genghis Khan and his successors.) When they returned to their home of Venice, Italy, the two brothers immediately planned a return journey. They had been invited by the Great Khan to return and bring 100 Christian missionaries and special oil from Jerusalem. After dealing for two years with church politics about sending missionaries, the brothers decided to leave anyway. In 1271, Niccolo and Maffeo began their second journey from Venice to the Far East. This time they took along 17-year-old Marco and two friars carrying letters from the Pope to the Khan. However, the friars became frightened and quickly abandoned the dangerous journey. They gave the letters to Marco to deliver instead.

The Polo expedition sailed from Venice to Acre (Akko), a port in Palestine, and went into Jerusalem to get the oil that the Khan wanted. They rode camels through Armenia where they saw petroleum and then saw the mountain believed to contain the remains of Noah's ark. Next, they traveled by ship to the Persian port of Hormuz in modern-day Iran. But the ships were not safe there, so the members of the Polo expedition continued to ride camels across deserts in Afghanistan where they saw ruby mines.

They rested one year in the mountains so that Marco could recover from a fever. Then they crossed the mountains of Tibet and traveled through the Gobi desert. In 1274, they finally reached Kublai Khan's summer palace in Shang-tu (Kalgan), where they received a rousing welcome. Marco claims he served the khan as a government official for 17 years. During this time, Marco said he visited the southern and eastern areas of China, Burma, Indochina, Indonesia, and Malaya.

Background Information *(cont.)*

In 1291, the Polos began asking the khan to allow them to go home. For a long time he denied their request. Finally in 1292, he let them leave to escort a huge bridal party to a relative in Persia (Iran). On their way, they were provided with 14 ships. They sailed to Singapore, then to Sumatra, and around the northern tip of India. The group traveled across the Arabian Sea and the Gulf of Oman to Hormuz. Sadly, most of the wedding party died on the trip. When they arrived in Persia, the groom had died, so the young bride married his son. The Polos traveled onward to the Turkish port of Trebizond (Trabzon) on the Black Sea. Next, they sailed to Constantinople (Istanbul) and finally to Venice, arriving in 1295.

When the Polo family arrived home, no one recognized them. Their own family had believed they had long been dead. Finally the family let them in and they had a great dinner. When all the servants had gone home, the three Polos opened up the hems of their tattered clothes and dumped out sapphires, diamonds, and other precious jewels. They brought back many luxurious gifts including ivory, jade, porcelain, and silk. Upon returning, they found Venice at war with Genoa. Marco took sides with Venice and was captured and imprisoned. Some scholars think he was on a ship that was captured. The prisoners were taken to Genoa.

During his jail sentence, he dictated his stories to his cell mate, Rustichello of Pisa, a popular romance writer. The handwritten book called *The Description of the World* was completed in 1298. The printing press had not yet been invented, so scholars rewrote the book by hand to produce more copies. In this book, Polo commented on many Far Eastern customs and the unique things that he had seen.

Did Marco Polo Really Travel to China?

Background Information *(cont.)*

Lying on his deathbed, Marco Polo was questioned again about his book in which he claims he traveled to China. Even back then there were people who doubted that he ever actually went on the journey that he wrote about. Marco proclaimed, "I have only told the half of what I saw." The book, which he wrote after his long journey to China, received mixed reviews. Some believed he had told wild tales. Many people in Venice called him "the man of a million lies." The information he left out of his book is what makes many question his journey today. But some people believed he told the truth. Even Columbus studied Marco Polo's book and used it to navigate a sea route to the Far East. Did he actually go to China or was his account a lie? Did he glean ideas about China from other travelers and then write about it as if he had taken the trip himself? Or did he really travel there, but merely exaggerated some of his stories to make them more interesting? Regardless of whether or not Polo actually traveled to China, his book changed the world by sparking European interest in the exploration of the Far East and eventually the exploration of a new world.

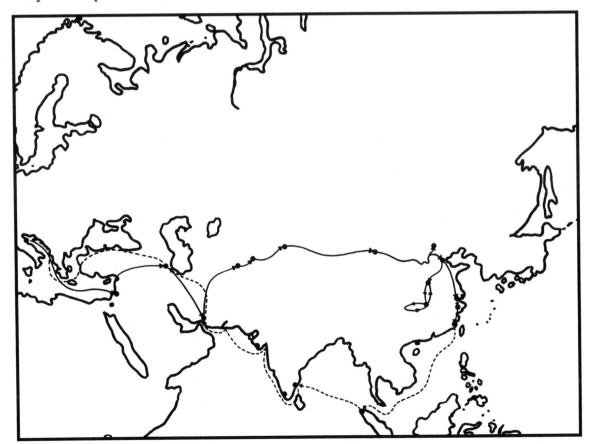

Did Marco Polo Really Travel to China?

The Prosecution's Case

Marco Polo is on trial for fraud. It is believed by the City-State of Venice, his home town, that he lied about his travels to China. We will prove that he did not go to China, but merely gained information about the Far East from other travelers. He used this information to make money by selling a book.

Prosecutor's Points

- In his book, Polo wrote about ridiculous things like seeing dog-headed men.

- He claimed that magicians in the Khan's court could make the cups of wine and milk fly in the air. He even said that Khan received his drinks without anyone having to carry them to him.

- He claimed to have learned four languages, but didn't say which languages.

- Marco also claimed that he ruled a province in China under the khan. Historical records in China from that time were meticulously kept, and Polo's name was missing from all of them.

- Polo also said he gave the Khan a gift of oil from Jerusalem and a letter from the Pope, but Chinese records failed to mention these gifts.

- Marco even said that he oversaw the building of catapulting machines that could throw 300-pound stones to fight in a battle, but the battle that he mentioned took place before the Polos even left Venice.

- He also described a famous bridge in Peking, which he said had 24 arches. It only has eleven arches.

- He never mentioned people eating with chopsticks, which was an unusual practice.

The Prosecution's Case *(cont.)*

Prosecutor's Points (cont.)

- He did not talk about seeing the Great Wall of China. It is believed he traveled near the Great Wall.

- The Chinese practiced cormorant fishing. A cormorant was a type of bird with a hooked beak. Fishermen would leash the cormorant and the bird would dive down and catch the fish. This was left out of his account.

- He did not talk about the beautiful Chinese writing of calligraphy.

- Paper was invented in China, but Marco did not think it was important enough to mention in his book.

- Women in China practiced foot binding to make their feet very small. This too is left out of his book.

- No diary or journal has ever been found with Polo's notes. There is no way he could have remembered everything that he wrote. He simply remembered what other travelers have said. He put that information together while he was in jail.

- After Polo died, his family was left with only a small amount of wealth. It did not equal the amount of wealth he claimed he found in China. Where did all the wealth go?

- On Polo's map, he used the Persian names, not the Chinese names. He learned these Persian names from other travelers. He did not include the Chinese names because he did not know them.

Did Marco Polo Really Travel to China?

Polo's Voyage Map

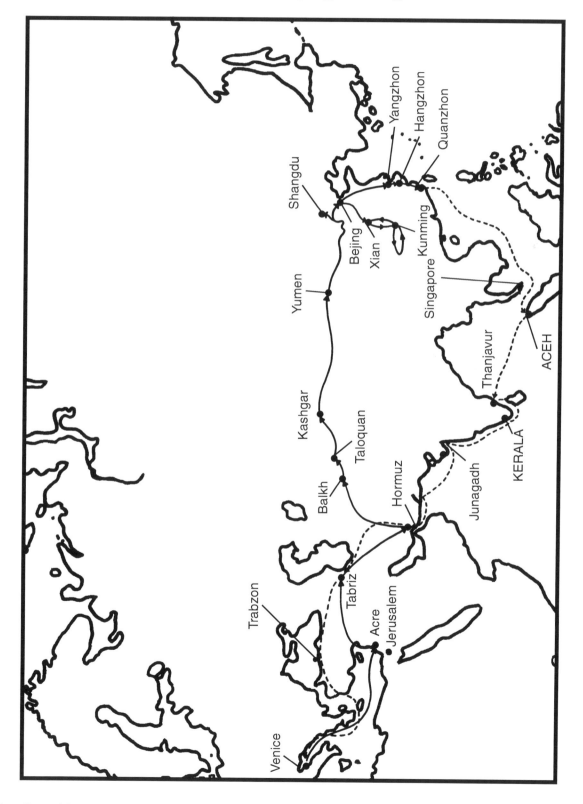

Did Marco Polo Really Travel to China?

The Defense's Case

Marco Polo is on trial for fraud. It is believed by the defense that Polo is innocent of these charges. This evidence will prove that he did make the trip to China.

Defense Points

- Most people can explain the exaggerated accounts like the dog-headed men by saying he liked to exaggerate his stories to make them more interesting. Others say that his ghostwriter, Rustichello, may be the one to blame for the exaggerations. What harm does a little exaggeration do if it makes the story more interesting?

- Polo mentioned that he saw black rocks that burn. Although we don't know it yet in Venice, Polo described hot coals.

- Polo did not mention paper, but he did mention paper money. Isn't that enough?

- Keep in mind, after so many years, Polo's memory was probably fuzzy on the details.

- There is no way that Polo would have known about the basic things in Chinese society because he did not mingle with the common people. His time was spent in khan's court and with royalty.

- Polo was not in Chinese records because the Chinese did not think it was important to write about a foreigner. They wanted to take all the glory for their own accomplishments.

- Polo would never have known about the practice of foot-binding because women who practiced this stayed indoors.

The Defense's Case *(cont.)*

Defense Points *(cont.)*

- Cormorant fishing was practiced more in the southern part of China, and Polo probably did not travel there.

- Even though the Great Wall was built long ago, it was in ruins by the time Polo went there. The area that Polo traveled to was probably an area where the wall had fallen.

- As Polo traveled east, he noticed people eating with chopsticks. By the time he got to China, it was not a strange site to him. He didn't think it was necessary to mention it.

- Polo did not need to learn Chinese because the Mongol script was used at the time. That script is similar to Arabic, which Polo knew.

Did Marco Polo
Really Travel to China?

Jury Vote

Directions: Each day you will have a chance to vote in the trial of Marco Polo. Will your vote change based on the evidence presented? Write your vote (guilty or not guilty) in the appropriate box.

Name: _____

Day 1 Vote:	Day 2 Vote:
Day 3 Vote:	Day 4 Vote:

Newspaper Headlines

Directions: In your opinion, did Marco Polo lie or did he tell the truth about his voyage to the Far East? Create a newspaper headline on this page that shows your opinion.

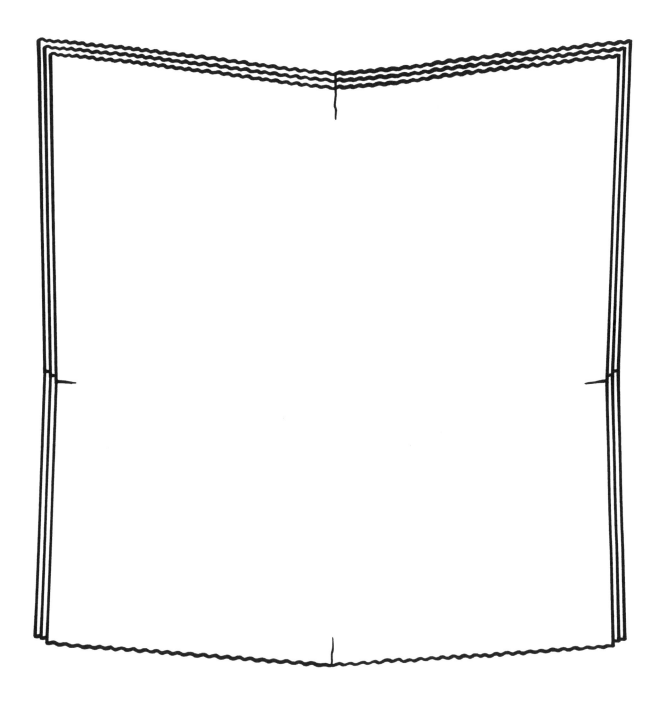

The Fingerprints of Shakespeare

Teacher Lesson Plan

Standard/Objective

✼ Explain why individuals and groups respond differently to their physical and social environments and/or changes to them on the basis of shared assumptions, values, and beliefs. (NCSS)

✼ Students will run one of four campaigns, create a visual representation of their candidate, prepare speeches, and vote in an election.

Materials

✼ copies of *Attention Grabber* (pages 39–41); *Who Was Shakespeare?* (page 42); *Graphic Organizer* (page 43); *Background Information* (pages 44–48); *Planning a Campaign* (page 49); *My Vote* (page 50)

✼ paper plates

✼ art supplies

✼ tongue depressors or craft sticks

✼ construction paper

Discussion Questions

✼ What is the meaning of your quote?

✼ Do you think these quotes could only be written by a well educated person?

✼ Give an example showing when someone would say one of these quotes.

✼ Who do you think wrote these famous quotes?

The Activity: Day 1

Make a copy of the *Attention Grabber* (pages 39–41) and cut out each quote. Put these quotes in a bag or basket and have each student draw one out. Tell students that they will be auditioning for a part in a play. They will audition using the quotes given to them, so they should think of a way to dramatize them. Give them a minute to read their quotes silently. Then begin the official audition, letting each student read his or her quote. At the end of the audition, let students cast a vote to choose the best actor.

Place students into four groups and ask the first three discussion questions above. Provide enough time for the groups to discuss each question. Then bring the class back together and ask the last discussion question. Some students might already be familiar with Shakespeare and his plays.

Explain that these quotes all come from plays written by Shakespeare. But, there is a huge controversy about Shakespeare's identity. Explain that there are some people who think that William Shakespeare did not really write these words. They believe another person authored his plays and sonnets.

Teacher Lesson Plan *(cont.)*

The Activity: Day 1 *(cont.)*

Place students back into their groups and give each group a copy of *Who Was Shakespeare?* (page 42). Read this aloud as a class. Distribute copies of the *Graphic Organizer* (page 43). Tell students that they will be using this page over the next few days to keep track of the candidates for authorship.

Then distribute a different *Background Information* page (pages 44–48) to each group. Each group will read one of the following: William Shakespeare (page 44), Christopher Marlowe (pages 45–46), Sir Frances Bacon (page 47), or Edward deVere (page 48). Explain that students should keep their information a secret for now. Have them fill in the information that they know on their graphic organizer.

The Activity: Day 2

Students will be creating a visual representation of their candidate and a speech for this candidate to deliver. Tell the class that they will be launching a campaign for authorship for their candidate. Allow students to gather back in their groups from the day before. Have students re-read the background information from the previous day. Explain that this person will be their candidate and they must have a visual representation of their candidate.

Half of the group will work on creating a visual representation of the candidate and the other half will work on a speech for their candidate.

Give each group a paper plate, large tongue depressor or Popsicle stick, construction paper, and art supplies. Tell students that half of their group will be making a candidate with these supplies. Let students have some class time to work on their art projects. You can suggest that students make the head using the paper plate and the tongue depressor should be stuck to the back of the plate to make it easy to hold. Students can bring other supplies from home if necessary.

Have the remaining students in each group work on a speech for their candidate. This speech should convince the audience that their candidate should be elected as the true author of Shakespeare's works. How will they use the facts in the background information about their candidate to convince the audience? Remind students that the other groups do not have access to their background information. They need to find a creative way to tell the information in their candidate's speech. The speeches will be presented to the class on the following day.

Teacher Lesson Plan (cont)

The Activity: Day 3

The candidates should be formally introduced to the class today. The teacher will read the speech to the class while the "candidate" stands nearby. After all the speeches have been presented to the audience, take a secret ballot poll. Have students write down the author they would choose based on the information in the speeches. Then announce the results of the poll at the end of class.

Have students gather back in their groups to decide on a campaign strategy. Distribute copies of *Planning a Campaign* (page 49). Each group should create at least one campaign poster and one campaign bumper sticker for their candidate. Both of these should have more than just the candidate's name. Challenge students to think of something short they can write on the poster and bumper sticker that will gain votes for their candidate. These can be displayed during the debate on Day 4 and throughout the rest of the week.

The Activity: Day 4

Explain that each candidate will participate in a debate today. Let each group select one person to speak as the "candidate" when asked the questions. Have each group submit four questions for the candidate to answer. Remind students that the questions should be about the authorship of Shakespeare's works.

Hold a debate with the teacher as the moderator. Allow each candidate to respond to each question, but give them a time limit of about one minute. At the end of the debate, take a secret ballot poll. Announce the poll results at the end of class.

The Activity: Day 5

Announce that this is election day for each candidate. Give each group enough time to create a two minute statement (or a last minute plea) from their candidate telling the audience why he should be chosen as the author of Shakespeare's works. Then have each "candidate" make his short speech.

Distribute copies of *My Vote* (page 50) to students and take a secret ballot vote. Remind students that they are voting based on the information presented about each candidate. Announce the winner and hold a victory celebration. During this celebration, let each group read their background information to the rest of the class. Ask the class if they think each group presented their information adequately during the campaign. Does any of this information change anyone's mind about the author of Shakespeare's works?

Attention Grabber

It is not in the stars to hold our destiny, but in ourselves.

Be not afraid of greatness: some are born great, some achieve greatness, and some have greatness thrust upon 'em.

Cowards die many times before their deaths. The valiant never taste of death but once.

To be, or not to be—that is the question.

Love all, trust a few, do wrong to none.

Love comforteth like sunshine after rain.

They do not love that do not show their love.

Oh! you gods, why do you make us love your goodly gifts, and snatch them straight away?

To thine own self be true; and it must follow, as the night the day, thou can'st not then be false to any man.

Defend your reputation, or bid farewell to your good life for ever.

Attention Grabber *(cont.)*

Good name, in man or woman, is the immediate jewel
of their souls.

The purest treasure mortal times afford, is spotless reputation.

Have more than though showest; speak less than thou
knowest; lend less than thou owest.

When sorrow comes, they come not single spies,
but in battalions.

Thus we play the fools with time; and the spirits of the wise
sit in the clouds and mock us.

To-morrow, and to-morrow, and to-morrow, creeps in this petty
pace from day to day, to the last syllable of recorded time.

It's not enough to speak, but to speak true.

The good I stand on is my truth and honesty.

Truth loves open dealing.

All the world's a stage, And all the men and women merely
players: They have their exits and their entrances; And one
man in his time plays many parts, His acts being seven ages.

Attention Grabber *(cont.)*

Friends, Romans, countrymen, lend me your ears!
I come to bury Caesar, not to praise him.

We are such stuff as dreams are made on.

Nothing can come of nothing.

The play's the thing.

Love looks not with the eyes but with the mind.

Our doubts are traitors, and make us lose the good we oft
might win, by fearing to attempt.

All that glitters is not gold.

How far that little candle throws his beams!
So shines a good deed in a weary world.

Neither a borrower nor a lender be;
For loan oft loses both itself and friend.

Give thy thoughts no tongue.

Who Was Shakespeare?

Who was the man that we call William Shakespeare? Very little is known about him and very few records exist. There are six handwriting samples from Shakespeare, and each time his name is spelled, it is spelled differently. Does this matter? Was he the man who authored so many popular plays that we now enjoy? Or did the author of these famous plays use the name "Shakespeare" to hide his or her identity?

The person who wrote Shakespeare's plays and sonnets must fit a list of characteristics. His plays are full of history, law, Latin, Greek, and knowledge of Italy and royalty. How could someone with only a grammar school education know so much and write so well? Was he simply a gifted writer who gained his knowledge by reading? If William Shakespeare of Stratford did not write the plays and sonnets, then who wrote them? Some theories include Edward de Vere (17th Earl of Oxford), Sir Francis Bacon, and Christopher Marlowe. Take a look at the most popular candidates.

Graphic Organizer

Directions: As you learn more about each candidate and their claims for authorship, write what you learn in the space below.

Stratfordians: William Shakespeare from Stratford

_____

_____

_____

Oxfordians: Edward de Vere from Oxford

_____

_____

_____

_____

Marlovians: Christopher Marlowe

_____

_____

_____

_____

Baconians: Sir Francis Bacon

_____

_____

_____

Background Information

The Case for William Shakespeare from Stratford

From the records that do exist, we know that William was born to an illiterate glove maker and wool trader named John Shakespeare in 1564 in Stratford-on-Avon. His mother could read and write, something uncommon in that day. During his early childhood, the Plague was raging through England. His mother had already lost two children to this disease, so she kept young William at home and indoors. William's father was elected to be an alderman, and it was customary that someone in that position could send his son to grammar school. If William did attend grammar school, then that is the only schooling he probably received.

The years of his 20s are considered the lost years. Some think that William was a schoolteacher in the country. There is one record in the countryside that does list a Shakeshafte as a young tutor. Others say he joined the military and others think he traveled to Italy during this time. Records show that when he was 18, he married Anne Hathaway who was eight years older. William and Anne had three daughters and one son. In the early 1590s, he left his family and moved to London. William's son, Hamnet, died at age 11. Scholars believed he wrote some of his best works after his son's death. He even mentions the grief of a child's death in one of the plays.

While in London, he acted with a group called the Lord Chamberlain's Men. They traveled and performed many plays for important people. Shakespeare's name appears on a list of actors who performed for the Queen. It is believed that during this time he was writing the plays that were performed.

When the Plague raged through London again, the theatre was closed to prevent the disease from spreading. Shakespeare then wrote his famous sonnets.

In 1594, the theatre group changed their name to the King's Men and acted for King James I. Shakespeare worked with others to have the Globe Theater built. He also owned part of the theatre.

When he was in his 40s, Shakespeare returned to Stratford and bought a large house. He died in 1616. His will did not mention any plays or poems. Seven years after William's death, his friends put together a compilation of his plays. This book was called First Folio. Plays were performed and not normally printed and published for the public. If it were not for these friends, these plays would probably have been lost forever.

Background Information *(cont.)*

The Case for Christopher Marlowe

Christopher Marlowe was the same age as Shakespeare. He was also a talented writer. Marlowe was recruited out of college to be a part-time secret service agent for the Queen. The Queen, a protestant, had to be protected from Catholic assassination plots. Marlowe wrote many works from London during this time. In May of 1593, he disappeared. Rumors began circulating saying that he was dead. He had actually been arrested on claims that he was an Atheist (a very serious crime in those days). He posted bail and then was free for about 10 days.

On May 30, 1593, Marlowe was at the house of a woman named Dame Eleanor Bull. Bull was a widow and to make money she rented out rooms in her house. Some think that her house was a safe house for government agents.

Four men were at the house that day. Robert Poley was a government agent and carried important letters for the queen. Ingram Frizer was a servant and personal business agent for Marlowe's boss at the agency. Nicholas Skeres was also a spy and frequently assisted Poley. While at this house, Marlowe was stabbed in the eye and died. The Queen was only 12 miles away at the time, so her royal coroner took care of reporting and recording Marlowe's death. The coroner said that there was an argument and that Frizer stabbed Marlowe in self-defense. Marlowe's body was quickly buried in an unmarked grave in a churchyard there. Frizer was implicated in the crime and he went to prison. Less than a month passed and the Queen pardoned Frizer. Frizer went back to work as a spy. Marlowe was only 29 years old. It appears that there might have been a cover-up about his death. Some say his murder was planned by the government.

However, some scholars believe Marlowe's death was faked. One theory states that he really did not die, but continued to live on and write under the pseudonym, Shakespeare. Many of Shakespeare's sonnets appear to be about his life. Amazingly, many of the topics of the sonnets describe Marlowe's life. These scholars believe Marlowe took a boat to France and then Italy on May 30. This would explain the many plays that include Italy as the setting.

Background Information *(cont.)*

The Case for Christopher Marlowe *(cont.)*

In the past few years, an interesting piece of evidence has become known. Anthony Bacon, the brother of Sir Francis Bacon, worked for the Earl of Essex. Essex was a member of the Queen's council. Two years after Marlowe's supposed death, Anthony Bacon introduced a Frenchman named Monsieur Le Doux to his boss, the Earl of Essex. Le Doux was a government spy. Le Doux sent letters to Bacon and one letter still exists today. This letter, signed Le Doux, strangely has the exact handwriting as Marlowe. Along with this letter is a list of 57 books that need to be paid for. The books include a French dictionary and French language phrases. (Why would a Frenchman need something like this?) Most importantly, many books on this list contain the plots from Shakespeare's plays. It is widely known that Shakespeare based his plays on popular stories or history. Could Marlowe have written these works and had his publisher distribute them in England?

Background Information *(cont.)*

The Case for Sir Frances Bacon

Sir Frances Bacon was a very smart man and a very good writer. He had attended Cambridge University, one of the best schools at the time. He was elected to the House of Commons. While working in government, he wrote proposals to settle the conflicts within England at the time. He is most famous for writing about science and philosophy. He came up with the idea of drawing conclusions based on a set of facts. He had powerful friends, including King James I.

Shakespeare's plays contain many references to the legal world. Bacon was a judge and a lawyer. However, the writings that are attributed to him lack the imagination that Shakespeare's plays contain. He wrote and published many books. With all the books that he published, would he have had the time to publish more than 30 plays and 156 poems? Bacon died in 1626 from bronchitis. In the 1800s, a woman named Delia Bacon claimed that Bacons' manuscripts were buried beneath Shakespeare's gravestone. However, she did not have the nerve to dig them up.

Others who believe Bacon was the true author say that the plays and sonnets are full of secret codes that reveal Bacon to be Shakespeare. For example, the First Folio divides the plays into categories. All the history plays are together and all the comedy plays are together. The word "bacon" appears on page 53 in both the comedy plays and the history plays. Some think this was how the author revealed his identity. . . Sir Frances Bacon. Another code example is the phrase from a Shakespeare poem:

> The Romaines plausibly did consent

> To Tarquins everlasting banishment.

If you take the first two letters of the last word in the second line: *ba*. Then if you take the first three letters of the last word in the first line: *con*. This reveals the word "bacon." Was the author trying to tell his readers something?

Background Information *(cont.)*

The Case for Edward de Vere, the 17th Earl of Oxford

Edward de Vere was recognized as a poet and playwright during his lifetime. Those who believe he was the author of Shakespeare's works point out that he had access to the Queen's court. He was the highest-ranking earl in the kingdom. In fact, he was the Queen's cousin. Many of Shakespeare's plays refer to royalty and the people and events that took place in the royal court. He traveled to Italy and even built a house there. Many of Shakespeare's plays take place in Italy. He graduated from Cambridge at just 14 years old and earned his master of arts at Oxford when he was 16. He then went to law school. While in his 20s, he wrote many poems. His writing seems to have vanished after that.

Some who believe he was Shakespeare say that he had to hide his identity. They say he did this because being a play writer was beneath the dignity of royalty. He also had to hide his identity because he revealed so much about the royalty and court. They certainly would not like knowing that someone in their court was writing about their faults for all the public to see. His family crest shows a lion shaking a spear. Even de Vere's secretary referred to him in a speech as a man whose "countenance shakes a spear."

His life has several strange coincidences with Shakespeare's play, *Hamlet*. De Vere's father died young and his mother remarried quickly. In the play, Hamlet's father dies very young and his mother remarries quickly. De Vere stabbed a servant and pirates captured him. Hamlet stabbed a man and pirates captured him. In another play, King Lear was a widower who had three daughters. De Vere was also a widower with three daughters.

His poems written in his 20s are not considered as good as Shakespeare's, but his writing style does resemble Shakespeare's. Many Shakespeare scholars say that the King's Men continued to produce new plays until 1614. When de Vere died in 1604, some of the best works of Shakespeare had not yet been published. This includes 15 of what some consider being his best works: *Macbeth, Antony and Cleopatra, The Tempest,* and *King Lear.* De Vere believers say that he wrote these plays before he died or that he at least started writing them and then someone else finished them. Others say that the recorded dates were not accurate and that the plays were actually written before 1604.

The Fingerprints of Shakespeare

Planning a Campaign

Directions: Use this page to organize your campaign. Your Party Name will be one of the following: Stratfordians, Oxfordians, Marlovians, or Baconians.

Party Name:_____

Candidate: _____

Slogan: _____

_____

_____

_____

Poster Design Ideas:

Bumper Sticker Design Ideas:

My Vote

Directions: Vote for the candidate who you think actually wrote Shakespeare's works. Then explain the reasons why you chose this candidate over the other three.

William Shakespeare ☐

Christopher Marlowe ☐

Sir Francis Bacon ☐

Edward de Vere ☐

My Reasons:

_____

_____

_____

_____

_____

_____

_____

_____

_____

Who Was the Man in the Iron Mask?

Teacher Lesson Plan

Standard/Objective

* Identify and use processes important to reconstructing and reinterpreting the past, such as using a variety of sources; providing, validating, and weighing evidence for claims; checking credibility of sources; and searching for causality. (NCSS)

* Students will analyze history, hear statements from eight different men, who all claim to be the Man in the Iron Mask, review evidence, and then make a judgment on his identity.

Materials

* copies of the *Attention Grabber* (page 55); *Background Information* (pages 56–57); *Graphic Organizer* (page 58); *The Writers Have Something to Say* (pages 59–60); *Death Certificate* (page 61); *Problems in the Family* (page 62); *The Mask* (page 63); *Suspects According to Historians* (pages 64–65); *The Guard Gives His Report* (page 66); *Finally, A Confession* (page 68)

* an overhead of *Roster of Prisoners in 1669* (page 67)

* poster board or large butcher paper

* markers

* black construction paper or cloth

* yarn

* hole puncher

Discussion Questions

* What is this letter about?

* Around what time in history did this mystery take place?

* Why do you think this man had to wear a mask?

* If given the chance, what do you think this prisoner would have said?

* Look at who wrote the letter and who the letter was addressed to. Why is this important to know?

The Activity: Day 1

Write the last three discussion questions listed above on large sheets of butcher paper or poster board using a marker. Hang these in three different places around the room. These will serve as brainstorming stations for students.

Teacher Lesson Plan *(cont.)*

The Activity: Day 1 (cont.)

Make copies of the *Attention Grabber* (page 55) and place them on the students' desks. If the mood strikes you, greet students at the door with a black velvet mask in front of your face. You can use the mask template found on page 63. Give them a few moments to read this letter and then have them choose partners. Ask the first two discussion questions above. Have students consult with their partners before answering. Then tell students that they will visit three brainstorming centers around the room to answer further questions about this mysterious letter. Let students walk around to each brainstorming center and write as many ideas as they can think of under the question using a marker. Encourage students to read the ideas already written before answering with their unique ideas.

Then distribute copies of the *Background Information* (pages 56–57) and let students read it with their partners. Take time afterward to talk about the information and to clarify any questions. Some students might have seen the movie or read a book about this topic. If so, warn students that the information in those sources might not be accurate, so they should keep an open mind when examining evidence.

Distribute copies of the Graphic Organizer (page 58). Tell students that they will use this page throughout the week to keep notes about each suspect.

The Activity: Day 2

Give students copies of *The Writers Have Something to Say* (pages 59–60). Remind students that just because something is in print, doesn't mean that it is the truth (with exception to official documents like the one they will examine today). Have students write down any new information on their graphic organizers.

Copy and distribute *Death Certificate* (page 61). This page will ask students questions according to the official death certificate of the masked man. Explain to students that this is a copy of the official certificate translated into English. Students can work with their partners or individually to answer questions on this page. Then have students refer back to their graphic organizers and eliminate or add other possible suspects to the list.

Just before class ends, select eight students who are willing to act as the Man in the Iron Mask on the following day. Tell them that they will receive further information tomorrow at the beginning of class. Distribute a copy of *The Mask* (page 63) to each volunteer and provide him or her with either black construction paper or black cloth to make the mask.

Teacher Lesson Plan

The Activity: Day 3

Provide students with a copy of *Problems in the Family* (page 62). Have students read it with their partners and then record information on their graphic organizers. Students will probably need to refer back to the background information from the day before. As students list the suspects on this page, have them give reasons for suspecting them as the masked man. Remind students to keep this page handy for the week because they will be constantly referring back to it and adding more information to it.

Provide each of the eight students with a different section from *Suspects According to Historians* (pages 64–65). Give them a moment to read through what they will say to the class. Set the stage by telling students that eight of the suspects have agreed to talk to them. But they will continue to wear their masks as they meet with them. You have chosen these suspects because historians who have studied this mystery think it could have been one of these men.

Have each suspect wear his or her mask. One by one call each suspect in front of the class. Have them read their statements before the class. After each one has read his or her statement, pause to talk about it as a class. Is there any real evidence in the statement that would implicate this person as the masked man? Or does it just make a good story? This is an important step for students as they learn to deduct real evidence. Who makes the list of more-likely-than-not suspects?

After all eight statements have been given, give students a few moments to record additional information on their graphic organizers. Students can ask each of the suspects to repeat their statements if necessary. Students can choose to disagree with the historians and continue to think it is another suspect that did not speak today. After all, there might be a little truth to some of these rumors.

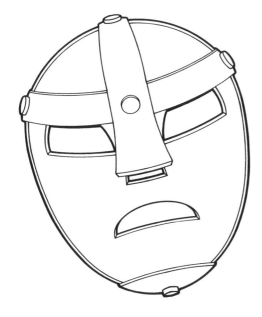

Teacher Lesson Plan *(cont.)*

The Activity: Day 4

Give students copies of *The Guard Gives His Report* (page 66). Have them read it with their partners and then record any important information on their graphic organizers.

Then explain to students that you have just received a copy of the roster of men who were at the Pinerolo prison. Ask students why this information would be important to the investigation. Have them look closely at the names. Place a copy of *Roster of Prisoners at Pinerolo in 1669* (page 67) on an overhead projector. Have students look at the names, and then look back at their graphic organizers. Does this information help their investigation?

The Activity: Day 5

Students must make a decision today on the identity of the masked man. Have them look back at their graphic organizers to refresh their memories. Then distribute copies of *Finally, A Confession* (page 68). Tell students to write the confession of the masked man, giving his name on this page. Then have them each cut out a mask from page 63 and tape it over his or her confession. Hang these in the room and have students take turns looking at each one.

Take a final moment at the end of class to talk about the identity. What helped each student to make his or her final decision? What does this tell us about examining evidence in a case?

1. Matthioli

2. Eustache Dauger

3. An insane Dominican monk

4. Dubreuil, who was arrested for spying

5. La Rivière, a servant of Fouquet, who accompanied his master to the prison

Attention Grabber

October 10, 1711

Dear Princess of Hannover,

. . . There was a man in the Bastille for several years, who had to carry a mask during every hour of the day. Two soldiers were constantly at his side with strict orders to kill him on the spot if he dared to take the mask off for a moment. He slept, ate and went to communion with the mask on. He even died in the mask. Even at the royal court his identity remained a mystery. . .

Sincerely,

Duchess Elizabeth Charlotte of Orleans, sister-in-law of Louis XIV

Who Was the Man in the Iron Mask?

Background Information

The Bastille is best known as a French prison. It was built as part of the fortified wall around the city of Paris in the 13th century. The government used it as a political prison during the 17th and 18th centuries. If the royal court decided that someone needed to be imprisoned, they issued a secret warrant and held the prisoner indefinitely without a formal charge or trial.

In 1698, King Louis XIV ordered a mysterious man to be imprisoned in the Bastille. This prisoner's identity was kept a secret. He was said to be tall with white hair and wore an iron mask (some say it was a black velvet mask) to conceal his identity. He had been a prisoner since 1669. He was first held in the fortress of Pinerolo. Then he was transferred to the Vauban Fort on the island of Sainte-Marguerite just off the coast of southern France. Finally, in 1698, he was transferred to Bastille. When he arrived, the government had to provide furniture for his room. Most prisoners at Bastille had the money to furnish their own rooms, but the government provided cheap furniture for those who were not well-to-do. On November 19, 1703, this prisoner died, but rumors about his identity continued for many years.

Most of the prisoners at Bastille during that time were people who had offended King Louis XIV. During the imprisonment at Bastille, there were two other masked prisoners besides this famous one. Why was this prisoner kept alive? If he knew some secret information, why wasn't he simply executed as many prisoners were at the time? For what reason was his identity concealed? If this prisoner spoke or showed his face to anyone, he would be executed on the spot. It is known that during that time of history, prisoners in Italy wore masks. Could this prisoner have been Italian?

And what would have offended this king? What was this king like? To answer these questions, it is important to know a little about his family history. The parents of King Louis XIV (14th) were King Louis XIII (13th) and Queen Anne of Austria. Historians say that they did not get along very well. After being married 23 years, they finally had a son, Louis, in 1638. Two years later they had another son, Philippe.

Background Information *(cont.)*

When Louis was just four years old, his father became deathly sick with tuberculosis. Before dying, he named his son, Louis, to be his successor. A man by the name of Cardinal Mazarin advised the Queen and her son. He became like a father to young Louis. In the meantime, Louis's brother, Philippe, was treated like a step-child. Both the queen and the cardinal were afraid that Philippe would outshine his brother, so they gave him a less-than-adequate education. Philippe was a very able military leader and possibly a very shrewd investor. He would have made a fine king.

Louis was forced to marry the King of Spain's daughter, Maria Theresa, for political reasons. He was a short man, but wore tall wigs and high heeled shoes to make himself look tall. When Louis was 22 years old, the Cardinal died and Louis was finally the sole ruler of France. He held that position for 72 years, the longest ruler in French history.

King Louis XIV chose people who were non-nobles to help him rule. Nobles might oppose his ideas or question his motives. He knew that to have power, he had to have absolute power. He has been described as a controlling, hardworking, and pleasant king, but he lacked self confidence.

Graphic Organizer

Directions: As you study this case, use this page to collect your evidence.

Who are the possible suspects?

Name	Evidence

The Writers Have Something To Say

In 1717, a great philosopher named Voltaire was imprisoned for about a year in Bastille. He claimed that he spoke with guards who had attended the Man in the Iron Mask. Voltaire published a book in 1751 called *The Age of Louis XIV*. He described the prisoner as young and handsome. He wore the finest clothing of lace and linen and spent time playing the guitar.

In Voltaire's later writings, he gave more clues about the identity of the prisoner. He said that the man looked like someone famous and was 60 years old when he died. The most famous man known at that time was King Louis XIV. Was he hinting that the Man in the Iron Mask looked like the king? If he really knew the identity, why did he not come out and tell the public? Or was he simply playing a joke on the public?

Another famous writer named Joseph de Lagrange-Chancel was imprisoned on the island of Sainte-Marguerite in the 1720s. He interviewed people at the prison that claimed that the governor of the island treated the masked prisoner very well and even called him "my prince." He was given linen to wear and offered the finest books. His meals were served on a silver platter. Quite a bit of time had passed since the prisoner was at that prison. Can these accounts be trusted as the truth?

In 1768, a descendant of the governor of the island wrote that the prisoner was called "Tower." He said that the prisoner only wore the mask in public and sometimes guards saw him without the mask. When in the presence of "Tower," prison officials removed their hats and showed deep respect for the prisoner. While in his presence, the prison officials remained standing until the prisoner gave them permission to sit.

The Writers Have Something To Say *(cont.)*

In 1789, a journalist named Frederic-Melchior Grimm wrote that he had talked with a servant in the royal household. This servant claimed that Louis XIV had an identical twin. Their father had worried that the boys would fight over the throne, so he sent the other boy away. He was raised in a nobleman's household in secret and was never told his true identity. When he was grown, he saw a portrait of his brother, King Louis XIV. He guessed he was his twin brother, and was immediately arrested. He spent the remainder of his life as the Man in the Iron Mask.

When the people of France rebelled against the King and stormed the Bastille on July 14, 1789, some writers claimed that the bones of the prince were there and the iron mask was still in place. Napoleon even believed he was a descendent of this prince.

Are all of these accounts fantastical stories, or is there some truth to them? It is up to you to be the judge.

Death Certificate

> November 19, 1703.
>
> Marchioly, about 45 years old, died in the Bastille; his body was entered on November 20, in the Cemetery of St. Paul, in the presence of Rosarges, major of the Bastille; and Doctor Reglhe, chief physician of the Bastille.
>
> Signed, Rosarges

Directions: Use the death certificate above and the background information you have read to answer these questions.

1. Describe the physical characteristics of King Louis XIV.

   _____

   _____

2. Describe the physical characteristics of the Man in the Iron Mask.

   _____

   _____

3. How old was the King at the time of the prisoner's death?

   _____

4. According to the death certificate, how old was the prisoner at the time of death?

   _____

5. Can this information eliminate any theory about the Man in the Iron Mask?

   _____

   _____

Who Was the Man in the Iron Mask?

Problems in the Family

Needless to say, King Louis XIV was not a very faithful husband. He fell in love with many women. One of them was named Louise de la Valliere, a friend of his brother's wife. He had two children with her, one of whom was rumored to be the Man in the Iron Mask. This child's name was Comte de Vermandois. Even though these children would never inherit the throne, the King was very generous with all his children.

Was Queen Anne a faithful wife? There are many people who don't believe that Louis XIV was really the son of Anne and Louis XIII. It was widely known that this couple hated each other fiercely. After all, it was 23 years before their first child was born. It was rumored that the queen was in love in a man by the name of Duc de Beaufort. Some believed that he was Louis XIV's real father, and that Beaufort was imprisoned as the Man in the Iron Mask to keep this secret from getting out.

Another similar story circulated about a man known by these initials: C.D.R. He, some claimed, was the Man in the Iron Mask. It was also rumored that Queen Anne loved the English Duke of Buckingham. Some think they had a son together and that this son was the Man in the Iron Mask. And it was also said that the Queen and the Cardinal had a son together, and the son was the Man in the Iron Mask.

Still another story suggests the Man in the Iron Mask to be the son-in-law of the queen's doctor. His name was Marc de Jarrigue de La Morelhie. Supposedly he had evidence that Louis XIV was not the King's true son, and he was imprisoned to keep his knowledge a secret.

The enemies of Louis XIV claimed that the King and Queen's first child was really a baby girl. They needed a boy to inherit the throne, so a boy was taken from someone else and raised as Louis XIV. The baby girl was sent away. When she grew up, people thought she was the Man in the Iron Mask. Those who believed this theory were enemies of Louis XIV and wanted to prove that he was not the rightful heir to the throne.

The Mask

Directions: Take this template and copy it onto black construction paper or black cloth. Using a hole punch, punch holes in the sides of the mask. Tie a piece of yarn threading it through each hole. Tie it tightly at the back of your head to hold the mask in place.

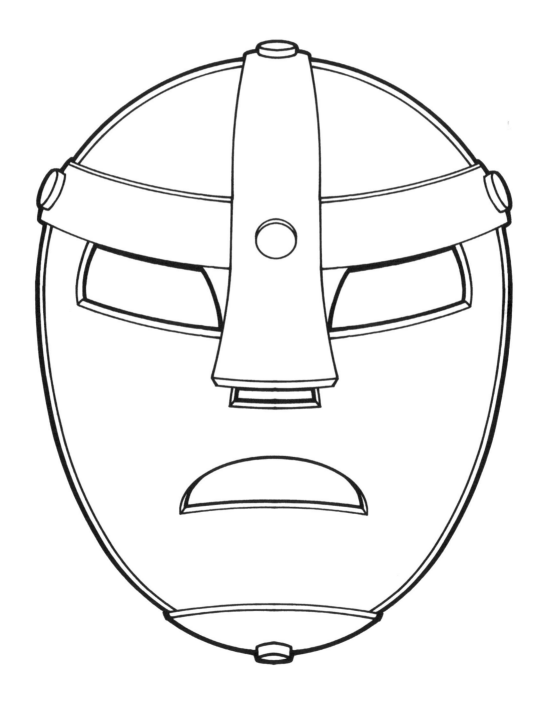

Who Was the Man in the Iron Mask?

Suspects According to Historians

The Duc de Beaufort: I am the Grand Admiral of France. I was killed in 1669 while fighting the Turks, but some believe that I was actually imprisoned in the iron mask because I, and not Louis XIII, was the real father of Louis XIV. However, there is no DNA evidence that can support or oppose this claim.

Eustache Danger: I am a servant who was arrested in 1669 along with my master, who was charged with high treason against Louis XIV. In recent times, some have speculated that the governor of the Bastille kept me in a mask simply to impress others with the fact that he had been entrusted with an important prisoner. It is known that I spent time in both Pinerolo and Bastille prisons.

Eustache Dauger de Cavoye: I am a French military officer who was arrested in 1668. Some believe I was arrested for participating in Satan worship. Some think the reasons for my arrest were kept secret because one of the King's mistresses was also a Satan worshipper. The King certainly would not have wanted her arrested! It is even believed by some that I was the illegitimate half brother of Louis XIV, which was why I was forced to wear the mask.

Nicolas Fouquet: I am the King's Minister of Finance. In 1661, the King attended a splendid fete at my mansion. My mansion was elaborately built and very beautiful. Everyone commented on it. Some think the king became so jealous of my mansion that he had me arrested. I died in prison in 1680. According to one story, the king had promised that year to free me, but changed his mind after learning that his current girlfriend had once been a girlfriend of mine. He didn't want to keep his promise to me, so he had my death staged. I really lived secretly as the Man in the Iron Mask.

Count Ercolo Antonio Matthioli: I am an Italian who worked as a secretary for the Duke of Mantua in Italy. The French wanted to buy the fortress of Casale from the duke, but I mishandled the negotiations. Louis XIV ordered me to prison. I wore a mask voluntarily because it was an Italian tradition for prisoners to wear masks at that time. I also spent time at the Pinerolo and Bastille prisons under the governor.

Suspects According to Historians *(cont.)*

Moliere: I am a famous actor and playwright. I died in 1673 of consumption, but some believe that my death was faked. I was imprisoned in the iron mask because the plays that I wrote offended religious people in power.

The Duke of Monmouth: I am the illegitimate son of Britain's King Charles II and the nephew of King James II. I was executed in London in 1685 for leading a rebellion against British King James II, my uncle. Some believe that James was unwilling to order his own nephew's death. Instead he had someone else executed in my place. He then sent me to prison in France in the iron mask.

The Comte de Vermandois: I am an illegitimate son of Louis XIV. I died of smallpox in 1683 at age sixteen. I died while in the military and many people saw me die. But some believed I did not die at all, but was taken away to prison and put in the iron mask for the crime of hitting the King's real son. Would my generous father do something like this to me?

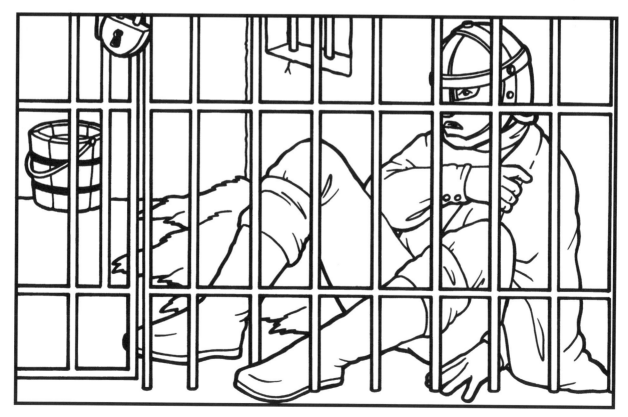

The Guard Gives His Report

Etienne Du Junca, the man second in command at Bastille, said that the prisoner wore a black velvet mask, not an iron one. From his writings, it seems that historians believe the mask was not an extra punishment for the prisoner. Could the mask have been to aid the prisoner in hiding his identity from everyone? In other words, did the prisoner not want people to know his identity? Junca wrote in his journal that he never saw the prisoner without that mask. He also said that the prisoner shared a room with two other common prisoners for a while. Wouldn't someone of great importance have his own room?

The guard reported that the prisoner was buried under the name, M. de Marchiel. In his journal he wrote: "Last night, November 19, at about ten o'clock, there died in his room the unknown prisoner, who has worn a black velvet mask since his arrival here in 1698. He had not complained of any serious illness, and the end came so suddenly that our chaplain was unable to administer the last sacrament . . . In the register his name was entered as M. de Marchiel, and the sum of money has been spent on the burial."

On the death certificate, the name is listed as Marchioly. Could the guard have just misspelled the name while writing in his journal? Was this name a cover-up name for the prisoner? Some historians think that it was his true name. If they had wanted to conceal his name with a false one, they probably would have picked a very common French name. Instead they used an Italian name.

Who Was the Man in the Iron Mask?

Roster of Prisoners at Pinerolo in 1669

1. Matthioli

2. Eustache Dauger

3. An insane Dominican monk

4. Dubreuil, who was arrested for spying

5. La Rivière, a servant of Fouquet, who accompanied his master to the prison

Who can be eliminated from the suspects list based on this evidence? Why?

Who Was the Man in the Iron Mask?

Finally, A Confession

Directions: You have finally cracked the case! The Man in the Iron Mask is ready to tell everyone his true identity. Write his confession in the space below. Then cover the confession up with your black mask. Secure the mask using tape at the top so that it can be flipped up from the bottom.

_____

_____

_____

_____

_____

_____

_____

_____

_____

_____

_____

_____

_____

Could Mozart Have Been Murdered?

Teacher Lesson Plan

Standard/Objective

❋ Work independently and cooperatively to accomplish goals. (NCSS)

❋ Students will look at four possible suspects who could have murdered Mozart, and then create skits that show the likelihood of each possibility along with death certificates that shows their final decisions regarding cause of death.

Materials

❋ copies of the *Attention Grabber* (page 72); *Background Information* (pages 73–75); *Graphic Organizer* (page 76); *Suspects Back Then* (pages 77–78); *Skit Ideas* (page 79); *Mozart's Symptoms* (page 80); *The Death Certificate* (page 81)

❋ Mozart's music

❋ dictionaries

❋ dark cloak

Discussion Questions

❋ What is a *requiem?*

❋ What kind of person would receive such a commission?

❋ Why would someone want a requiem written?

❋ Why do you think the person did not want his identity known?

The Activity: Day 1

To set the mood, play Mozart's *Requiem* in the background. If possible, wear a dark cloak and distribute copies of the *Attention Grabber* (page 72) to students as they enter class. Act very mysterious and tell students that they are not allowed to ask questions about your identity. (This attention grabber describes the commission that Mozart received just months before his death. The stranger Mozart spoke with about the commission did not permit Mozart to ask who commissioned the funeral music. It did not take long for the mysterious circumstances to convince Mozart that he was writing this for his own funeral.)

Provide students with dictionaries to look up the definition of a *requiem.* Then ask the discussion questions above. Create brainstorming lists on the board as students give answers to these questions. Finally, tell students that the man who received this commission was Mozart, and he died four months after receiving this commission.

Could Mozart Have Been Murdered?

Teacher Lesson Plan *(cont.)*

The Activity: Day 1 (cont.)

Distribute copies of the *Background Information* (pages 73–75) and read it aloud to the class. Remind students that it is not known for sure if Mozart died from natural sickness or if he was poisoned (murdered). They will be looking at all possibilities, including the idea that Mozart died of natural causes. This activity will help students to think deeply about circumstantial evidence and factual evidence.

Distribute copies of the *Graphic Organizer* (page 76). This page asks students to sift through all possible suspects using the Background Information. Students will continue to record any information about the cause of death on this page throughout the week. Have students find a partner. They should work together to complete this page.

The Activity: Day 2

Before class begins, copy *Suspects Back Then* (pages 77–78) and cut apart the suspect descriptions. Refresh students' memories about Mozart and the information that they read the previous day. Ask students if they think that Mozart was poisoned. Take a vote and put the results on the board.

Write the words "circumstantial evidence" and "factual evidence" on the board. Ask students to explain what each of these phrases mean. If necessary, provide dictionaries and have students look up the words *circumstantial* and *factual*.

Divide students into four groups. (If your class is large, divide it into eight groups.) Give each group a different suspect from the *Suspects Back Then* page. (If you have eight groups, two groups will represent each suspect.) Have each group read about their suspect. Explain that they will be presenting the information to the rest of the class in a skit. It is the goal of each group to prove that their suspect poisoned Mozart. Distribute copies of *Skit Ideas* (page 79) to groups. Give students the rest of the time to come up with a skit for their suspects. Students might also want to bring in props for their skits, which will be presented the following day.

The Activity: Day 3

Give students a few moments to practice their skits. Then have each group present their skit to the class. At the end of each skit, allow the presenting group to explain the theory about their suspect and show how their skit was based on circumstantial evidence. It is important that students understand that most of these suspicions are based on circumstantial evidence, and not hard facts. Finally, take a vote to see what students think about the suspect. Keep a tally on the board.

Could Mozart Have Been Murdered?

Teacher Lesson Plan *(cont.)*

The Activity: Day 4

Distribute copies of *Mozart's Symptoms* (page 80). This page gives a little more information on the possibility of natural causes of Mozart's death. Let students talk about it and compare the likeliness of natural causes to the possibility of murder. Ask students, which one seems to be more likely? Take a vote. Compare that vote to the previous votes.

Then distribute copies of *The Death Certificate* (page 81). Students will write their final opinions on this certificate. Post these death certificates on a bulletin board and let students read what their peers wrote. If possible, end the study with students listening to some of Mozart's music.

Mozart's Symptoms:
high fever, sweating, abdominal pain, vomiting, swollen feet and hands, rash

Possible Causes:
Pneumonia frequently produces fever and delirium as the lungs fill up with fluid.
Kidney failure could produce delirium and eventually poison the body.
His wife did say on one occasion that the doctors bled him. If a patient has kidney problems, bleeding him or her could prove to be deadly. Doctors did not know this at the time. Mozart might have been prescribed mercury for his high fever. When a patient is given mercury, he often experiences tremors, dementia, and drooling. While some think that Mozart could have been delirious, no one reported that he had tremors or drooling.

Certificate of Death

Name	Wolfgang Amadeus Mozart
Date of Birth	January 27, 1756
Place of Birth	Salzburg, Austria
Date of Death	December 6, 1791
Cause of Death	

_____

_____

_____

_____

Attention Grabber

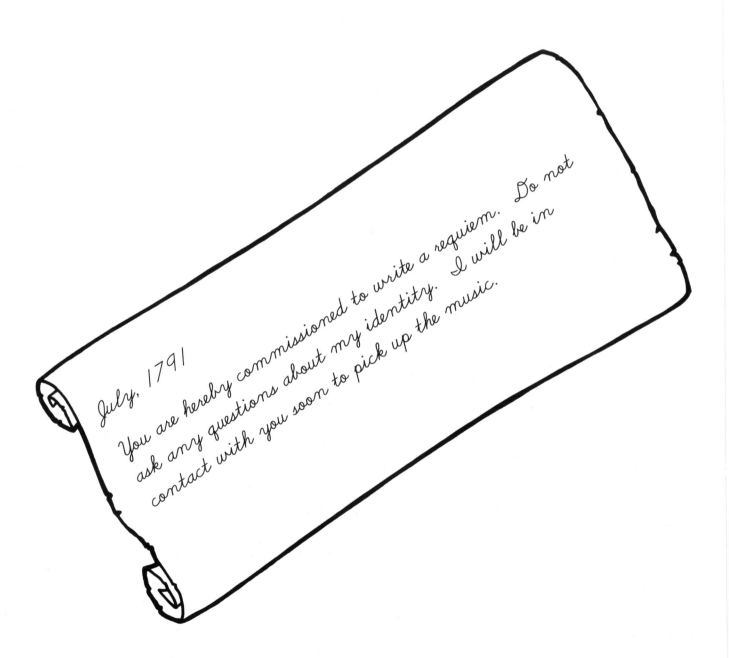

July, 1791

You are hereby commissioned to write a requiem. Do not ask any questions about my identity. I will be in contact with you soon to pick up the music.

Could Mozart Have Been Murdered?

Background Information

Mozart was born in Salzburg, Austria on January 27, 1756. He had six siblings, but only one sister survived childhood. His father, Leopold, was a musician, too, and had just written a book about playing the violin when Mozart was born. He earned extra money for his family by teaching violin lessons. Even Mozart's mother came from a long line of musicians. Leopold was a talented musician, but he was not as talented as Mozart.

Mozart spent his time watching his older sister play the harpsichord. A harpsichord looks like a piano, but when a key is pressed down, a string is plucked like a harp. No one bothered to teach Mozart because they thought he was too young to learn. When his sister finished playing, Mozart made his way to the bench and played beautiful music. He was only three years old! He learned by listening to the notes. Mozart began writing music when he was five years old. His parents soon realized that they had a prodigy, a child genius, on their hands.

Musicians at that time were sponsored by wealthy merchants, clergy, and royalty. Traveling was a way that these sponsors could gain popularity. They allowed their musicians to take time off to travel, and in return, the musicians would promote their sponsors. So, his father arranged to take seven-year-old Mozart on a tour to show off his amazing talents. Leopold took Mozart and his sister on a three-and-a-half year tour. Along the way, people gave them expensive gifts like coins, watches, and clothing. Mozart dressed like a little man wearing a wig and carrying a sword at his side.

Many speculate that Mozart's childhood caused most of his sickness as an adult. In fact, Mozart was sick much of the time while on these trips. He overcame scarlet fever and his sister narrowly escaped death after having typhoid fever. Both he and his sister contracted small pox, too. They survived, but the disease left scars on their faces.

Traveling at that time was difficult, especially for children. They rode in horse-drawn carriages on bumpy dirt roads. Sometimes these carriages broke down. It was expensive to travel, too. Much of the money they earned paid for their lodging and food. They slept in strange beds crawling with fleas and ate whatever food was given to them. They had to constantly be aware of thieves hiding on these roads.

Could Mozart Have Been Murdered?

Background Information *(cont.)*

When Mozart was 12, he composed his first opera. An opera is much like a play, except the words are sung instead of spoken. He traveled in Italy and wrote operas for people there. By the time he was 17, his sponsor made him come back to Salzburg. When he was 21, he quit working for his sponsor in Salzburg and traveled to Paris to find work. His mother went with him, but died there.

A few years later, Mozart tried unsuccessfully to get the position of court composer in Vienna. Another musician named Antonio Salieri already had that position. Antonio was six years older than Mozart. Some think that they were rivals. Salieri did not go on to be famous, except for the fact that he was one of Beethoven's music teachers.

Mozart married a girl named Constanze. Their first baby died and so did three more. Only two boys lived. To get through the sadness of losing his children, Mozart buried himself in his work. He produced popular operas, but unfortunately, no one could pay him. His family struggled financially.

In an effort to make money, Mozart joined the Freemasons in Vienna in 1784. He hoped that some wealthy members would pay him to compose. Mozart soon found out that many members were just common people. Freemasons believed that all men were created equal. This belief made the royalty angry, and they shut down many Freemason lodges. They saw the revolution happening in the colonies and became afraid that the common people in Europe might try to overthrow their throne in a revolution.

Mozart composed music for the Freemason's special ceremonies. One composition was called *The Magic Flute*. The story is about a queen who asks a prince to rescue her daughter from a magician. The prince is given magical instruments including a flute and some bells. The magician turns out to be a wise man. He took the girl away from her mother, an evil queen. The magician did this so that the girl would marry the prince. Despite its simple story, the composition was a huge success with the public. In this opera, Mozart revealed some secrets about the Masonic ceremonies, including their initiation rites. The opera also was full of Masonic symbolism, like the continual use of the number 3. The Freemasons had rules that punished a person with death if he revealed any secrets. The opera was performed more than 100 times in Vienna. Mozart hoped that this opera would put the mysterious Masons in a good light in people's eyes. Even though the opera was popular, the King completely outlawed Freemasonry in Austria three years later.

Could Mozart Have Been Murdered?

Background Information *(cont.)*

Mozart relied on the Freemasons financially. He also gave music lessons to children from wealthy families. Within a few years, Mozart was busy again writing an opera for the king's coronation. The money began rolling in. He had so many deadlines that he frequently worked himself sick. Then he would recover and continue working.

In July of 1791, a mysterious man knocked on Mozart's door. The man was a messenger and was dressed in a gray cloak. He asked Mozart to write a requiem. A requiem was music for a funeral. He told Mozart that he would be paid well, but he was not to ask about who ordered the music. To Mozart, this man was the messenger of death. Mozart soon became convinced that he was writing this requiem for his own funeral. Unknown to Mozart, a wealthy Viennese named Count Franz Walsegg-Stuppach ordered the music to honor his dead wife. This wealthy man frequently hired composers to write music, and then he would pass the music off as his own compositions. This information was unknown to Mozart, and he was consumed with writing this requiem.

In the meantime, Mozart's health began to deteriorate. He spent more time in bed. Sometimes his hands would swell. The doctors reported that he had a rash on his body. As his sickness worsened, he complained that his enemies were poisoning him. Some thought he was delirious at this point. His sickness in the past was caused by kidney problems and infections in his body. He died at his home on December 6, 1791.

He completed two out of eight sections of the requiem, but left a sketch of the rest. Just before he died at the age of 35, Mozart told one of his students how to finish it. This student and a few others finished the masterpiece. It has been played for years and was the piece of music selected to honor the victims of September 11th.

Could Mozart have been murdered? Anything is possible. Mozart was buried in an unmarked grave, so it would be difficult to find and identify the body. There was no autopsy performed to determine the cause of his death. In addition, the death certificate is missing. The question to whether he was murdered cannot be answered with certainty. The answer to this mystery will forever remain unknown.

Could Mozart Have Been Murdered?

Graphic Organizer

Directions: How good of a detective are you? How well do you look for clues? Do you speculate on all possible solutions? Look at the Background Information pages. When Mozart was sick in bed, he suspected that someone was poisoning him. After his death, his wife and others speculated that someone could have poisoned him. We do not have the medical evidence to prove that Mozart was poisoned—but we do not know for sure how he died. What if Mozart was murdered? Who could be a suspect?

Name of Suspect	The Motive

Could Mozart Have Been Murdered?

Suspects Back Then

Directions: Cut along the dotted lines on this page and page 78 to make four sections. Divide the class into four groups. Give each group a different section. Each group will need to create a skit showing that the suspect could have poisoned Mozart.

What about Franz Hofdemel? The day of Mozart's funeral, Franz Hofdemel attacked his wife. His wife was one of Mozart's students. After attacking her with a razor and cutting her face, Franz then killed himself. It was rumored that he had something to do with Mozart's death. It was also rumored that his wife and Mozart were in love, but there is no evidence to support this claim.

What about Salieri? In the 1820s (30 years after Mozart's death) it was rumored that Antonio Salieri confessed to poisoning Mozart. Beethoven's son, Karl, and another man wrote about it in one of Beethoven's conversation books. Conversation books were used to communicate with the deaf.

In fact, Salieri accused himself of poisoning Mozart in 1823. However, he was diagnosed as senile at that point. Was Salieri jealous of the young Mozart, or was Mozart jealous of him?

Suspects Back Then *(cont.)*

What about the Freemasons? Did they conspire to poison Mozart for revealing their secrets? They had rules that punished people by death if their secrets were revealed. Were they angry with Mozart for composing *The Magic Flute?* After Mozart's death, they held a ceremony to honor him. They even printed the speech written for his funeral. We know that a fellow Mason helped Mozart with this opera. We also know that this fellow Mason was not punished in any way. With the Masons receiving so much persecution from the royalty, some think Mozart wrote the opera to improve their image in the eyes of the public.

What about Mozart's doctors? Some doctors today believe that if Mozart was murdered, his doctors were to blame. In hope of helping Mozart, his doctors could have helped him die. We do know that Mozart had kidney problems. The common practice at that time was to bleed a patient. Bleeding a patient would have made his kidney problems worse.

Another practice at the time was to prescribe mercury for extreme fever. We do not know if his doctors prescribed mercury. We know today that mercury is poisonous.

Skit Ideas

Directions: Create a skit to prove your suspect poisoned Mozart. Write your ideas in the space below.

Characters in the skit:

_____

_____

_____

Scene(s) that you will show:

_____

_____

_____

In your group's opinion, why is it likely that this suspect poisoned Mozart?

_____

_____

_____

How is this theory based on circumstantial evidence?

_____

_____

Props you will need for your skit:

_____

_____

_____

Could Mozart Have Been Murdered?

Mozart's Symptoms

Even though the death certificate is missing, we do have some first-hand accounts about Mozart's symptoms from the doctors and his visitors.

Mozart's Symptoms:

high fever, sweating, abdominal pain, vomiting, swollen feet and hands, rash

Possible Causes:

Pneumonia frequently produces fever and delirium as the lungs fill up with fluid.

Kidney failure could produce delirium and eventually poison the body.

His wife did say on one occasion that the doctors bled him. If a patient has kidney problems, bleeding him or her could prove to be deadly. Doctors did not know this at the time.

Mozart might have been prescribed mercury for his high fever. When a patient is given mercury, he often experiences tremors, dementia, and drooling. While some think that Mozart could have been delirious, no one reported that he had tremors or drooling.

The Death Certificate

Directions: You have reviewed all possible causes of death for Mozart. How did he die? Was he murdered? Below is a death certificate. Write what you think in the space below.

Certificate of Death

Name   Wolfgang Amadeus Mozart

Date of Birth   January 27, 1756

Place of Birth   Salzburg, Austria

Date of Death   December 6, 1791

Cause of Death

_____

_____

_____

_____

Beethoven's Love Letters

Teacher Lesson Plan

Standard/Objective

* Identify and use processes important to reconstructing and reinterpreting the past, such as using a variety of sources; providing, validating, and weighing evidence for claims, checking credibility of sources; and searching for causality. (NCSS)

* Acting as detectives, students will piece together clues about Beethoven's Immortal Beloved and make an educated guess as to her identity.

Materials

* copies of the *Attention Grabber* (pages 85–87); *Graphic Organizer* (page 88); *Background Information* (pages 89–91); *Clues in the Letter* (pages 92–93); *The Candidates* (pages 94–96); *The Portrait* (page 97); *Extra Thoughts on the Candidates* (page 98); *Beethoven's Itinerary* (pages 99–100); *Signed, The Immortal Beloved* (page 101)

* Post-it® Notes

* Beethoven's music

Discussion Questions

* What kind of letter is this?

* Who wrote this letter?

* Who was the letter written to?

The Activity: Day 1

Before students come into class, make copies of the *Attention Grabber* (pages 85–87). This is a love letter written by Beethoven. Fold the letter and then tape one under each desk. Have students close their eyes and listen to the following scenario that you will read to them.

Scenario: Your sadness is so great that you can hardly stand it. It was just yesterday that Beethoven died. He was a great composer, but he was also your brother. You sigh. At least you don't have to be in here alone. Beethoven's two friends have come to help you search his apartment. You know the papers are in here somewhere. More than 10 years ago, your other brother died. He left behind a son named Karl. These papers, or bank shares, will help your nephew, Karl. Beethoven had willed these bank shares to him, and you are in charge of finding those papers. You investigate everywhere, looking, hunting, exploring. As you search his cabinet, you are suddenly aware that there is a secret compartment underneath. You yell to Beethoven's friends that you have found something. You carefully open it up. First, you pull out a portrait. You look on the backside to see if there is a name or a dedication. There isn't. You and your brother's friends are not sure if you know this woman. Next, you pull out a letter and open it. Surprisingly, it is addressed to you and your other brother. Hmmm. It was written about 25 years ago.

Teacher Lesson Plan *(cont.)*

The Activity: Day 1 *(cont.)*

Scenario: (cont.)

You think back to that time and realize Beethoven had been struggling with the loss of his hearing. He wrote it from the small town of Heiligenstadt. You reach under the cabinet into the small compartment one more time and feel around. What do you find? Is there something else there? Yes, there is. Take it out and open it. (At this time instruct students to take out the letters hidden underneath their desks.)

Ask the discussion questions from the previous page. Tell students that they will be working in detective teams to solve the mystery presented here. Each team of detectives will work to identify the woman Beethoven called his Immortal Beloved. Ask students to work in their teams to brainstorm a list of things they know about Beethoven. Then have each team share their information aloud.

The Activity: Day 2

Divide students into small teams of 2-4 people. Explain that these teams will act as detectives. For the next few days they will be presented with evidence. The job of each team is to examine the evidence and categorize it on a chart. Distribute a copy of the *Graphic Organizer* (page 88) to each team. Explain that detectives use organizers like this to keep track of their evidence and to see how it all ties together. Give each team a large sheet of poster board or butcher paper and some Post-it® notes. Students will reproduce the graphic organizer on this large paper. They will write their notes about the case on the Post-it® notes and place them in the correct columns. Provide a place in the room for each team to hang their graphic organizer.

First, each team needs to know a little bit about Beethoven. Distribute copies of the *Background Information* (pages 89–91) and let students read about Beethoven in their teams. Then let students write the clues about Beethoven that they feel are relevant to the case on their Post-it® notes and place it under The Letter column on their large graphic organizer clue board. To help with this investigation, distribute a copy of *Clues in the Letter* (pages 92–93) to each team.

The Activity: Day 3

Distribute copies of *The Candidates* (pages 94–96) to each team. Have them work together to find relevant clues and writing Post-it® notes for their clue boards. They also might want to paste the women's pictures on the clue board. Then distribute *Beethoven's Itinerary* (page 99–100) and let students put together more information on their clue boards. Encourage students to look for clues as to where he was and where each woman was when the letter was written.

Teacher Lesson Plan *(cont.)*

The Activity: Day 4

Before class, copy *The Portrait* (page 97) for each team and cut it up to resemble a puzzle. Place the pieces from each puzzle into separate bags so that each team will have one puzzle.

Begin by having the teams piece together their puzzles. You might want to play some of Beethoven's music in the background for an added effect and to help students become familiar with this composer. When the puzzles are complete, let students tape their puzzles together.

Ask the discussion questions below. Be sure to explain to students that they will need to use their creativity when answering the second question. For the last question, you might want to tell students that they are listening to music written by Beethoven.

- What does your puzzle show?
- Who could this woman be?
- How old is this picture?
- What does this woman have to do with the music you hear playing in the background?

Distribute *Extra Thoughts on the Candidates* (page 98). Students will again make Post-it® notes about these clues for their clue boards.

The Activity: Day 5

Give students a few minutes to review their information on the clue boards. Then distribute copies of *Signed, The Immortal Beloved* (page 101). Students are to use the information that they have gathered on their clue boards and decide on the identity of the Immortal Beloved. Then they will compose a letter to the public from the Immortal Beloved. Her name should be signed at the bottom. Post these letters for everyone to read. As a final activity, you might have students tally the results of everyone's investigations.

Attention Grabber

The Letter (part 1)

July 6, in the morning

My angel, my all, my very self—Only a few words today and at that with pencil (with yours)—Not till tomorrow will my lodgings be definitely determined upon—what a useless waste of time—Why this deep sorrow when necessity speaks—can our love endure except through sacrifices, through not demanding everything from one another; can you change the fact that you are not wholly mine, I not wholly thine—Oh God, look out into the beauties of nature and comfort your heart with that which must be—Love demands everything and that very justly—thus it is to me with you, and to you with me. But you forget so easily that I must live for me and for you; if we were wholly united you would feel the pain of it as little as I—My journey was a fearful one; I did not reach here until 4 o'clock yesterday morning. Lacking horses the post-coach chose another route, but what an awful one; at the stage before the last I was warned not to travel at night; I was made fearful of a forest, but that only made me the more eager—and I was wrong. The coach broke down on the wretched road, a bottomless mud road. Without such tools as I had with me I should have remained stuck in the road. Esterhazy, traveling the usual road here, had the same fate with eight horses that I had with four—Yet I got some pleasure out of it, as I always do when I successfully overcome difficulties—Now a quick change to things internal from things external. We shall surely see each other soon; moreover, today I cannot share with you the thoughts I have had during these last few days touching my own life—If our hearts were always close together, I would have none of these. My heart is full of so many things to say to you—ah—there are moments when I feel that speech amounts to nothing at all—Cheer up—remain my true, my only treasure, my all as I am yours. The gods must send us the rest, what for us must and shall be—

Your faithful LUDWIG

Attention Grabber *(cont.)*

The Letter (part 2)

Evening, Monday, July 6

You are suffering, my dearest creature—only now have I learned that letters must be posted very early in the morning on Mondays to Thursdays—the only days on which the mail-coach goes from here to K.—You are suffering—Ah, wherever I am, there you are also—I will arrange it with you and me that I can live with you. What a life!!! thus!!! without you—pursued by the goodness of mankind hither and thither—which I as little want to deserve as I deserve it—Humility of man towards man—it pains me—and when I consider myself in relation to the universe, what am I and what is He—whom we call the greatest—and yet—herein lies the divine in man—I weep when I reflect that you will probably not receive the first report from me until Saturday—Much as you love me—I love you more—But do not ever conceal yourself from me—good night—As I am taking the baths I must go to bed—Oh God—so near! so far! Is not our love truly a heavenly structure, and also as firm as the vault of heaven?

Attention Grabber *(cont.)*

The Letter (part 3)

Good morning, on July 7

Though still in bed, my thoughts go out to you, my Immortal Beloved, now and then joyfully, then sadly, waiting to learn whether or not fate will hear us—I can live only wholly with you or not at all—Yes, I am resolved to wander so long away from you until I can fly to your arms and say that I am really at home with you, and can send my soul enwrapped in you into the land of spirits—Yes, unhappily it must be so—You will be the more contained since you know my fidelity to you. No one else can ever possess my heart—never—never—Oh God, why must one be parted from one whom one so loves. And yet my life in V is now a wretched life—Your love makes me at once the happiest and the unhappiest of men—At my age I need a steady, quiet life—can that be so in our connection? My angel, I have just been told that the mail coach goes every day—therefore I must close at once so that you may receive the letter at once—Be calm, only by a calm consideration of our existence can we achieve our purpose to live together—Be calm—love me—today—yesterday—what tearful longings for you—you—you—my life—my all—farewell. Oh continue to love me—never misjudge the most faithful heart of your beloved.

ever thine

ever mine

ever ours

Beethoven's Love Letters

Graphic Organizer

Clue Board

The Letter	
When was the letter written?	
Where was the letter written?	
Where was the letter's destination?	
The Candidates	
Antonie Brentano	
Josephine Brunswick	
Anna Marie Erdödy	

Beethoven's Love Letters

Background Information

Ludwig van Beethoven was born in Bonn, Germany, in the year 1770. The exact date of his birth was not recorded, but he was baptized on December 17. Back then most babies were baptized within a day or two of birth. At a very early age, Beethoven showed promise as a musician. His greedy father pounced on that idea and planned concerts for the young Beethoven to showcase his talent. The father of Mozart had done the same thing and had made money at it. No doubt, Beethoven's father wanted to do the same thing. To make Beethoven's talent seem even more amazing, he told the public that his son was two years younger than his actual age.

Musical talent ran in the family. Beethoven's grandfather had been an exceptional musician. His father was a singer, but did not possess the extraordinary talent of his son, Ludwig. Others recognized that Beethoven had talent, too. People encouraged him to develop this talent and offered to pay for his piano lessons. Even Mozart commented on the future of the younger Beethoven. Beethoven went to Vienna as a teenager with the hopes of studying under the great Mozart, but had to return home when he received news of his sick mother.

Beethoven's mother died soon after, so he stayed home and helped raise the family. His two brothers were under his watchful care for a few years. His father's drinking caused him to be irresponsible and to mistreat Beethoven.

By his early 20s, Beethoven was performing for many wealthy people. But Beethoven did not like being treated like a servant. He wanted to be treated as an equal, something that was difficult for wealthy people to do back then. For this very reason, Beethoven had trouble finding work. He often would storm out if others ordered him around. Beethoven was much like any man back then. He wanted to marry and have children. He wrote letters to friends admiring that they had found the loves of their lives.

Beethoven's Love Letters

Background Information *(cont.)*

Shortly before Beethoven turned 28 years old, he started having trouble with his left ear. He noticed a strange buzzing sound. Then it moved to his right ear. For many years, he consulted doctors hoping that they could cure this hearing problem. To this day, no one knows for sure why Beethoven lost his hearing. Some speculate that even doctors today would not be able to cure the problem.

During the autopsy after his death, the bones inside his ear called the ossicles were removed. The doctor planned to examine them later. They were never examined and were finally lost. If these bones were found, we might know today why he went deaf. Today, doctors think that his hearing loss was due to one of two things. The first is that the auditory nerve could have been damaged. This damage could cause the complete hearing loss. The other option is that the ossicles inside his middle ear became thick. As they thickened, they became fixed in one place. The ossicles conduct sound through the middle ear. If ossicles won't let sound through, the person cannot hear.

Beethoven was distraught at the thought of losing his hearing and tried to keep this illness a secret. His letters to friends tell of his frustration with these doctors. Beethoven easily became impatient and suspicious of those trying to care for him. His doctors thought it was best that he move to a quiet place in hopes of curing his deafness. It was during this time, in 1802, that he was sent to the quiet village of Heiligenstadt. Just before moving back to Vienna, he wrote out a letter to his brothers. This letter is called the "Heiligenstadt Testament." In this letter, Beethoven poured out his feelings to his brothers. He talked about his frustration with his illness, and mentioned what he would like them to have in the case of his death. Within 10 years, he was completely deaf.

In 1817, he started using conversation books to communicate with others. He could still talk, but was unable to read lips and did not have any other way to understand those around him. They would write what they were thinking in the conversation books and he would answer them back aloud. There were more than 400 of these books, but most were burned by his personal secretary after his death. His secretary explained that he burned them because many of the conversations were about politics, and that was a touchy subject at the time. He did not want Beethoven's reputation to be ruined.

Beethoven's Love Letters

Background Information *(cont.)*

In 1811 and 1812 he made a trip to Teplitz during the summer months. He had suffered from intestinal problems and doctors thought the water treatments there might help him. Teplitz was known for its spas. The spas did not seem to help his stomach and Beethoven found himself frustrated with his doctors again.

Beethoven's later years were plagued with more stomach sickness. Beethoven gained custody of his nephew Karl and spent the last 10 years taking care of him. Beethoven finally died, March 26, 1827, from cirrhosis of the liver. Thousands mourned his death and attended his funeral. He never married or had children of his own.

The day after Ludwig van Beethoven died, his brother and two friends went through his papers trying to find the bank shares he left to his nephew, Karl. Suddenly they stumbled upon a secret compartment in a cabinet. In the compartment, they found two letters and a picture of a woman. One letter was addressed to Beethoven's brothers. It was the "Heiligenstadt Testament" he wrote while in Heiligenstadt. The other letter had no name, but it was a love letter written by Beethoven. It was addressed to someone he called his Immortal Beloved. Who was this Immortal Beloved? Was she the same woman in the portrait?

Why did Beethoven have the letter in his possession? Did he not send it? That is a small possibility, but he wrote it over two days. It wasn't as if he rashly wrote a letter and then changed his mind on mailing it. Another possibility is that he demanded the letter back from the woman. It is also possible that he had an argument with her and she gave it back to him out of spite.

Many scholars have ideas on who this woman was, but no one can say for sure. Beethoven was a private man. While he did not openly share his feelings with his friends, we do know that he did love several women throughout his lifetime. Some letters have survived, but none as passionate as this letter.

Clues in the Letter

Proving when the letter was written

The letter was written on Monday, July 6. What year was it written? July 6 falls on a Monday during the following years: 1795, 1801, 1807, 1812, and 1818.

He writes that he lives in Vienna ("V" in the letter), but was not in Vienna when he wrote the letter. He did not live in Vienna in 1795, 1801, or 1807. In 1818, Beethoven had custody of his nephew Karl, It is unlikely he would have had time for anything else except taking care of his nephew.

He also wrote that he was taking baths. These were no ordinary baths; they were medical treatments. In 1811–1812, these baths in the waters of Teplitz were prescribed by his doctors.

Proving where the letter was written

Where was Beethoven on July 6–7, 1812? Beethoven's signature on the registry provides the proof that he was in Teplitz on July 7, 1812 for water treatments.

Where was the Immortal Beloved when Beethoven wrote the letter?

First, what places did Beethoven mention in his letter? Because Beethoven frequently abbreviated in his letter, this makes this question a challenge. Beethoven mentions V and K.

V stands for Vienna. No one disputes this fact.

K is where the Immortal Beloved was at the time the letter was written. Beethoven is concerned that the letter gets to K.

What is K? K could stand for Karlsbad, which is 100 km from Teplitz. K could also be Klosterneuberg, which is 10 km north of Vienna.

Clues in the Letter *(cont.)*

Beethoven did go to Karlsbad at the end of July, but was this planned at the time he wrote the letter? Beethoven said in the letter that they would see each other soon.

On July 17, 1812, Beethoven wrote a letter to a little girl named Emilie. In that letter he thanked her for the wallet she made him. He told her to write to him there in Teplitz where he would be for four more weeks, or in Vienna. The year before, his schedule was exactly the same. He stayed in Teplitz for a treatment, and then went home to Vienna. There are also letters Beethoven wrote to his publishers. He asked them to mail his music to him there in Teplitz or in Vienna. Would Beethoven have told these people to mail him there if he had not planned on being there? Is that enough evidence to prove that his trip away to Karlsbad was unexpected and sudden?

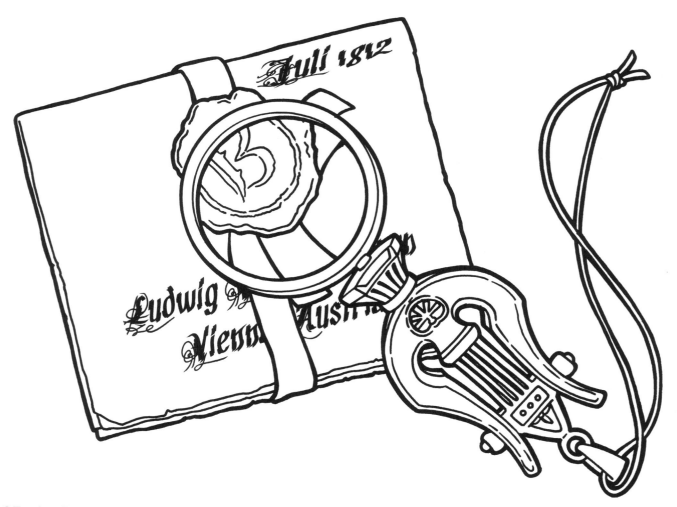

The Candidates

Antonie Brentano (1780–1869)

Her Statement:

Some people call me Toni. I met Beethoven in 1809. We developed a very close friendship with each other at that time. I lived in Vienna from 1809 to 1812. I was married and had one child at the time. My husband was a close friend of Beethoven's, too. Beethoven did write us, but we never met face to face again after 1812.

In 1811, Beethoven wrote a song called, "To the Beloved." I wrote the words, "Requested by me from the author on March 2, 1812" in the corner of the manuscript.

I was in Prague at the same time as Beethoven during 1812. I also traveled on to Karlsbad where Beethoven went at the end of the month. He stayed in the same guesthouse as my family and I did.

The Candidates *(cont.)*

Josephine Brunswick (1779–1821)

Her Statement:

My family met Beethoven in 1799. I was married at that time, but my husband died in 1804. I lived in Vienna until 1808. Beethoven was in love with me and waited a year after my husband's death to form a close relationship. As you probably know, it is proper to allow the person to grieve over a lost loved one for a year. I am sure that Beethoven hoped to marry me someday. He wrote passionate letters to me during that time. I could not marry Beethoven, because my children needed stability and a good income. Beethoven had not yet begun making a large income. My family pressured me to marry Count Van Stackelberg in 1810, but it was a very unhappy marriage. While I did not talk with Beethoven after 1807, when I broke his heart, he did keep close communication with my family. My husband and I separated after just a few years. I was living in Vienna in 1812.

Beethoven's Love Letters

The Candidates

Anna Marie Erdödy (1779–1837)

Her Statement:

In 1796, I married Peter Erdödy, but he abandoned our children and me after a few years. We had three children in all. During the years of 1808 and 1809, Beethoven had a room in my house located in Krugerstrasse. He visited my family often on my estate near Vienna. I am a good pianist, and I loved Beethoven's works. I even hosted his concerts in my home. Beethoven dedicated several compositions to me.

In 1809, Beethoven and I had an argument that strained our relationship. Being the suspicious man that he was, Beethoven heard rumors that I was in love with his personal servant. I had secretly given his servant extra money. I did this because Beethoven could be extremely difficult on his servants if things were not cleaned perfectly. He wanted his sheets to have no wrinkles and to be perfectly white. I wanted this servant to continue working for Beethoven and thought the extra money would entice him to stay. But Beethoven believed the rumors, not me. He quickly moved out of my house, and we did not speak for almost a year. By fall of 1811, we were on speaking terms, and forgiveness was granted on both sides. He moved again to be close to my home near Vienna in a small town called Hernals.

The Portrait

Directions: This portrait was found among Beethoven's belongings after his death. Who is this woman and is she his Immortal Beloved? Compare her photo with other women Beethoven knew from that time.

Extra Thoughts on the Candidates

Antonie

Why would Beethoven have written, "remain my true, my only treasure, my all as I am yours" if Antonie was already married? Divorces in Europe were very unlikely at that time in Europe and had to be granted by the government. Beethoven was a good friend of Antonie's husband. Would Beethoven love a person if she were the wife of his good friend?

Josephine

There is a difference between the letters Beethoven sent to Josephine and the love letter in question. Beethoven wrote in German, and the German language has two different ways to address someone: one is very formal and proper; the other is very personal and shows a very close and warm relationship. Beethoven addressed Josephine in a very formal way. In the love letter, Beethoven addresses the person in a very personal way.

Was Beethoven still in love with her during the time that she was married? Did he have hopes that her marriage would end?

Anna Marie

The closest post office to Hernals was in Klosterneuberg, and that is where Anna Marie sent and received her mail.

In regards to the servant incident: Was Beethoven upset because she had given his servant money, or was he upset because he loved her and did not want her to love anyone else?

Beethoven's Love Letters

Beethoven's Itinerary

Directions: Where was Beethoven during the summer of 1812? This may give a clue to whom he would see and where he would see his beloved. Track his route on the map on the following page.

June 28 or 29 — Beethoven left Vienna for Teplitz

July 1 — Beethoven arrived in Prague

July 2 — Beethoven met with friend, Karl Varnhagen

July 3 — Brentanos arrived in Prague on their way to Karlsbad, Beethoven missed his arranged meeting with Varnhagen

July 4 — Beethoven left Prague

July 5 — Arrived in Teplitz at 4:00 A.M.

July 6 & 7 — Beethoven wrote the love letter

July 19–25 — Beethoven met with friend, Goethe

Left Teplitz somewhere in between

August 6 — Beethoven performed in a concert in Baden

August 7 — Beethoven traveled with Brentanos from Karlsbad to Franzensbrunn

September 8 — Beethoven returned to Karlsbad and met friend, Goethe

September 16 — Beethoven was back in Teplitz, became ill, and was tended by a singer named Amalie Sebald

Beethoven's Love Letters

Beethoven's Itinerary *(cont.)*

Late September   Beethoven traveled to Hernals right outside of Vienna. He wrote a letter to his publishers from there.

October   Beethoven returned to Teplitz for a while, then left and visited his brother in Linz.

November   Brentanos left Vienna and moved to Frankfurt, Beethoven returned to Vienna.

Map

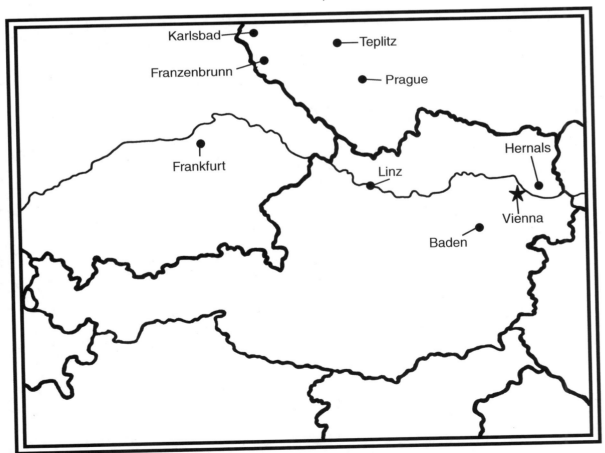

Beethoven's Love Letters

Signed, the Immortal Beloved

Directions: Your investigation has been quite a success. You have gathered clues and have finally made a decision on the woman's identity. Imagine you are the Immortal Beloved. In the space below, write a letter to the public unveiling your identity and "sign your name" so that everyone will finally know the truth.

The Mystery of the Mary Celeste

Teacher Lesson Plan

Standard/Objective

✳ Identify and use processes important to reconstructing and reinterpreting the past, such as using a variety of sources; providing, validating, and weighing evidence for claims; checking credibility of sources; and searching for causality. (NCSS)

✳ Students will create stamps that shows their theories of what happened to the *Mary Celeste.*

Materials

✳ a copy of *Ghost Ship Simulation* (page 106)

✳ copies of the *Attention Grabber* (page 105); *Graphic Organizer* (page 107); *Background Information* (pages 108–110); *Pirate and Mutiny Theories* (page 112); *Explosion and Weather Theories* (page 113); *Briggs and* Dei Gratia *Conspiracy Theories* (page 114); *A New Stamp for* Mary Celeste (page 115)

✳ copies or overhead of the Mary Celeste *Route* (page 111)

Discussion Questions

✳ What do you think happened to the ship?

✳ Look closely at the picture. Does this ship look like it was in good condition?

✳ Each of these stamps represents a theory. Can you define each theory according to the stamp?

✳ What is your theory?

✳ Is your theory included on one of these stamps?

The Activity: Day 1

Begin by reading the *Ghost Ship Simulation* (page 106) to students. Have them close their eyes and imagine that they are seeing what you are describing. When you get to the end of the simulation, distribute copies of the *Attention Grabber* (page 105) to students. Ask the students first two discussion questions above as they look at the picture. Students should realize that the ship is not in good condition in this picture. Point out that the sails are torn and flapping in the wind.

Then distribute copies of the *Graphic Organizer* (page 107). Students will be keeping track of the different theories of the *Mary Celeste* crew disappearance on this page. Tell students that they will be referring to this page throughout the week. Have students study these stamp pictures. Explain that each of these stamps depicts a theory about what happened to the crew of the *Mary Celeste.* Ask the remaining three discussion questions.

Finally, distribute copies of the *Background Information* (pages 108–110). Have students find friends and take turns reading this information together. Distribute copies of the Mary Celeste *Route* (page 111) or make an overhead of this page so that students can reference the route that the *Mary Celeste* sailed while they are reading.

Teacher Lesson Plan *(cont.)*

The Activity: Day 1 (cont.)

Tell students to look for more theories about the crew disappearance in the *Background Information* and then create more stamps for the *Graphic Organizer* page. They will be creating stamps based on different theories each day after their investigations.

Then bring the class back together and see if there are any further questions about the *Background Information*. Make a separate list of those unanswered questions on the board or on an overhead. Some of these questions may be answered as students investigate this week.

The Activity: Day 2

Students should form small groups (two or three per group). These small groups will be private-investigator firms. Let each group name their firm.

Explain to each firm that the United States Post Office wants to print a new stamp commemorating the crew of the *Mary Celeste*. The post office wants this mystery solved once and for all. Tell students that their firms have been chosen to investigate this mystery and then provide a stamp supporting their investigation. The stamp must show what really happened to the crew of the *Mary Celeste*. They will create this stamp only after they have completed a thorough investigation. Explain to students that for the next few days they will be investigating this mystery for the USPS.

Distribute copies of *Pirate and Mutiny Theories* (page 112). Explain to students that these are two separate theories. Have each investigative firm work together to answer the questions on this page about the theories. Students should first work on the pirate theory and then work on the mutiny theory. Have students refer back to their graphic organizers and add a stamp for these theories if there is not one already in their stamp collection. At the end of each investigation students will give each theory a score of likelihood. A "1" is the lowest score and it means that the theory is not likely. A "10" is the highest score and means that the theory is highly likely.

Teacher Lesson Plan *(cont.)*

The Activity: Day 3

Distribute copies of *Explosion and Weather Theories* (page 113). Explain to students that these are two separate theories. Have each investigative firm work together to answer the questions on this page about both theories. Students should first work on the explosion theory and then work on the weather theory. Have students refer back to their graphic organizer pages and add stamps for these theories if they do not yet have them in their stamp collections.

The Activity: Day 4

Distribute copies of *Briggs and Dei Gratia Conspiracy Theories* (page 114). Explain to students that these are two separate theories. Have each investigative firm work together to answer the questions on this page about both theories. Students should first work on the Briggs conspiracy theory and then work on the *Dei Gratia* conspiracy theory. Have students refer back to their graphic organizer pages and add stamps for these theories if they do not yet have them in their stamp collections.

The Activity: Day 5

Let each investigative firm meet back together to consult with each other on their investigations. They should make a final decision regarding what happened to the crew of the *Mary Celeste*. Students should look back at their graphic organizers to refresh their memories. They should also look at the scores they gave each theory. Tell students that a final theory can be a new theory not already presented, but must have reasons to support it.

Distribute copies of *A New Stamp for Mary Celeste* (page 115). Give students time to create their stamps. Then, if time permits, let each firm present their theory and show their stamp.

Attention Grabber

Ghost Ship Simulation

You rock back and forth with the motion of the ship on the water. You've been at sea for several weeks and haven't seen another ship since you left New York. Back and forth, back and forth. The sea never gets tired of tossing the ship. You look up and notice the sails are torn and shredded. You look down and see a red stain on the board of the ship. Is that blood or wine? You can't remember. You look over at the rail and notice a small gash in the wood. How long has that been there?

As you wonder about these things, you look out onto the sea and suddenly something takes your breath away. It's a ship in the distance! They put up the sails that mean they can offer help if you need it! You begin jumping up and down on the deck and excitedly waving your hands.

As the ship draws near, you hear the captain's voice in a speaking trumpet similar to a megaphone. He is offering you a greeting. You yell back.

The ship comes closer and you squint to see three sailors get into a rowboat. It seems like it takes years for them to reach you. When the men come aboard, they ignore you. You try and talk to them, but they look right past as if they are searching for something else. They inspect every part of the ship, and you are so frustrated. You hear them asking, "What happened to the crew?" You try and tell them, but they keep talking as if they don't hear your explanations. After being on board for a little while, the men leave and go back to their own ship. You plead and beg for them to take you, but they continue to ignore you. Why didn't they hear you? Suddenly it dawns on you. They are not ignoring you. They can't see or hear you because you are simply a ghost.

Graphic Organizer

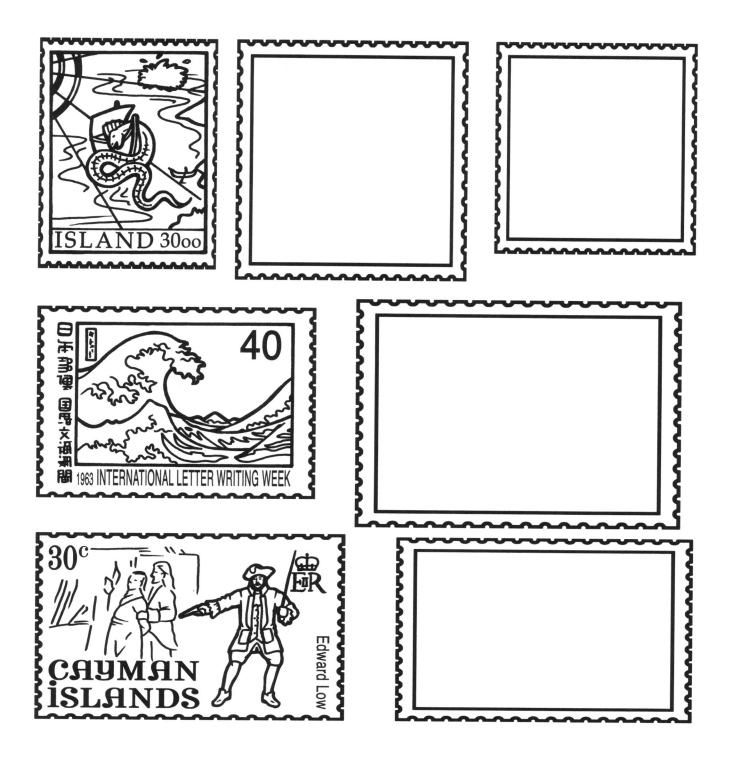

The Mystery of the Mary Celeste

Background Information

More than 125 years ago, a crew from a ship named the *Mary Celeste* mysteriously disappeared without a trace about 600 miles from Portugal. Nothing appeared to be stolen. No blood was found anywhere on the ship. How could something like that happen? Who, if anyone, was to blame? Although many people have theories about what happened, this mystery has never been solved.

The mysterious disappearance was not the first time the ship had bad luck. This ship was built in 1861. She was about 100 feet long. A beautiful scroll decorated the front of the ship. She was first named *Amazon* and used for transferring goods between countries. Just nine days after setting sail for the first time, her captain, Robert McLellan, died of pneumonia. The ship was given another captain who crashed the ship between Maine and Nova Scotia. As the hull was being repaired, a fire broke out on the ship. That captain lost his job. While on her way from London to France, the third captain crashed her into another ship. In 1867, the bottom of the ship scraped the ground, and she was sold for a very low price. After she was repaired, she was renamed the *Mary Celeste*. The new owner hoped that giving a new name would release the ship of her bad luck.

In November 1872, Captain Benjamin Briggs prepared the ship to travel from New York to Europe. Briggs was an honest man and came from a family of sailors. He had lots of experience sailing and had already served as the captain of three other ships. The ship carried many cases of raw alcohol. Raw alcohol was used in Italian wines. No one on board would be tempted to drink raw alcohol because any person who drank it would fall into a coma. Briggs took along his wife and two-year-old daughter and a crew of seven men. He left his seven-year-old son behind in America because his son was in school.

They left the harbor on November 5, but after setting sail in bad weather, the captain docked the ship along the shore for two days. When the weather calmed down, they set sail for Italy.

On December 5, the crew from the ship *Dei Gratia* spotted a ship coming towards them. They waited and very soon could see that the ship was in trouble. It swayed back and forth in the water and two of its sails were gone. They wondered, did the crew on this ship commit mutiny? Or was everyone drunk below deck? The sailors strained to see any clues through their spyglass.

The Mystery of the Mary Celeste

Background Information (cont.)

Finally, David Morehouse, the captain, ordered three sailors to investigate the mysterious ship. Deveau, Johnson, and Wright boarded the tiny rowboat and paddled over. As they searched the ship, they found that it was empty. The lifeboat was missing and the hatch, the largest opening in the deck of the ship, was wide open. There was very little seawater on the ship, so it was not in danger of sinking, and if they had encountered a storm, it would have been safer to stay on the big ship rather than in a life boat. In addition, the wheel was not tied to a specific course, which caused the ship to rock back and forth and go in all directions.

Down below they noticed the captain's cabin. It appeared that his daughter had been sleeping in the bed and several of her toys were on the floor. His wife's jewelry was still there along with all their clothing. A musical instrument and books of music were still on a shelf. A bag of dirty clothes was in the bathroom and an old dress hung nearby with a pair of old shoes underneath.

When they inspected another cabin, they discovered the ship's log book. The last entry was made on November 25 at 8 A.M. As they read the entries, they could not find any warning signs or problems listed. The sailor's pipes and tobacco were still there.

The galley where the crew met for meals was cleaned up with enough stored food and fresh water for six months. Pots, pans, and utensils were cleaned and put away. Nothing was missing. One of the sailors said that there was no alcohol at all in the galley.

Despite the tidiness of the ship, there were a few important things missing. . . things that a ship rarely left shore without. The chronometer was relied upon because it kept accurate time. Motion and weather did not affect it. It was missing. The sextant is an instrument that sailors use to navigate by tracking the stars. It was also missing. A navigation book is filled with charts so that sailors know how to find their way through the waters. This too was missing. The ship's register, which lists the specifics about a ship along with its owner, was gone. It is possible that these things were left behind in New York, but most captains had these things on board.

In the cargo hold, all the barrels of raw alcohol were unopened and intact. Each barrel was made from red oak. Red oak barrels allow some fumes to escape, but there was no sign of an explosion or of any smoke damage.

Background Information *(cont.)*

The three men rowed back to tell their captain the news. The captain of the *Dei Gratia* was a good friend of Captain Briggs. He was very sad to hear the mysterious news. Just before the trip, he had dinner with Briggs. The laws of the sea said that the ship belonged to the *Dei Gratia* now, and they knew they would get lots of money for the ship and the cargo.

Three crew members sailed the *Mary Celeste* to Gibraltar. When the *Dei Gratia* arrived there with the *Mary Celeste*, they learned that the government believed that the crew of the *Dei Gratia* was to blame. It was believed that the crew might have killed the crew members of the *Mary Celeste* and taken over the ship. The crew was taken to court.

The attorney general brought three small pieces of evidence against Morehouse. He noticed a small gash in the ship's railing. He also noticed that Brigg's sword had a few places of rust on it. He believed these spots were blood. He thought it was suspicious that the last log entry showed the ship far from where Morehouse told them he had found it. This evidence was not enough to convict the crew and they were eventually cleared from any wrong doing. They only collected one-fifth of the value of the *Mary Celeste*, which was not very much money considering they had to pay their own court costs out of it.

Over the years, many have tried to offer solutions to this mystery. This same naval inquiry that tried Morehouse and his crew tried to come up with a solution to this mystery. They could not find any explanation for what happened to the crew of the *Mary Celeste*. Morehouse said that he believed the fumes from the raw alcohol caused an explosion in the cargo area. He thinks this explosion caused the crew to abandon ship, but there is no evidence of damage to the ship. If there was an explosion, it would have been a very small one. Some think a sea monster attacked the crew or that a UFO took them away. Others believe that the crew caught some sort of deadly sickness or that pirates attacked the ship. Most people don't rule out that the crew could have mutinied or been killed by a large storm.

It is unlikely that the truth will ever be known. The *Mary Celeste* was finally wrecked and left in the Atlantic. Although the old and decaying ship was rescued in the past few years, no clues remain that haven't already been examined. It appears that the mystery will never be solved for sure.

Mary Celeste Route

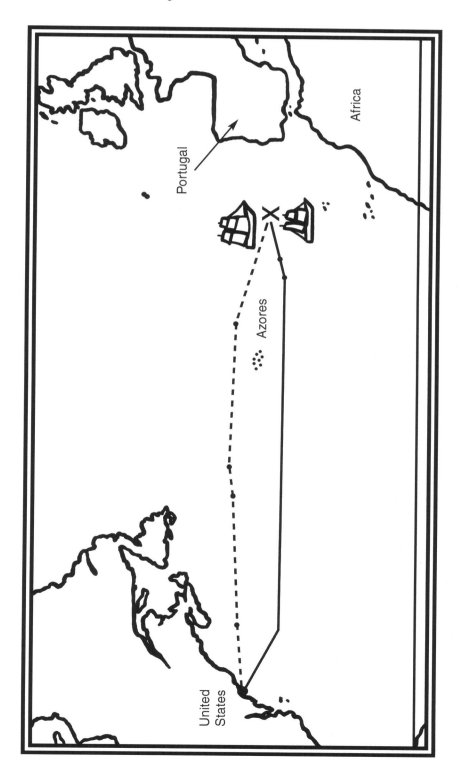

Pirate and Mutiny Theories

Directions: Look at each investigation below separately. Answer the questions, refering back to the background information and your graphic organizer page for answers. Then make a judgment about the theory based on a scale of 1 to 10 with 10 being the most likely (highest) theory and 1 being the least likely (lowest) theory.

Pirate Theory

Pirates caught up with the *Mary Celeste* and took control of the crew. They forced the crew off the boat. At that point, the crew might have left in the life boat. They could have been killed and thrown overboard. Or they might have been forced to walk the plank and drowned in the water.

Questions:

- Are there any clues that hint to a fight on board the ship?
- What valuables were found on the ship?
- Were any valuables taken? How do you know?
- Is there a record book that lists all the valuables taken aboard the ship?

Likelihood Score:

Mutiny Theory

The crew was a rowdy one. The captain thought he could keep them in line, but he was wrong. They first got drunk. Then they mutinied and killed the captain and his family. They took the lifeboat and rowed away to safety.

Questions:

- Was there alcohol that the crew could drink on the ship?
- Was any of the alcohol from the cargo tampered with?
- What valuables were taken from the ship?
- Would the things missing from the ship have been enough for the crew to survive on while on the lifeboat?
- Why did the crew abandon the ship?

Likelihood Score:

Explosion and Weather Theories

Directions: Look at each investigation below separately. Answer the questions, refering back to the background information and your graphic organizer page for answers. Then make a judgment about the theory based on a scale of 1 to 10 with 10 being the most likely (highest) theory and 1 being the least likely (lowest) theory.

Explosion Theory

The crew suddenly heard a noise like a large explosion in the cargo area of the ship. When this happened, a hatch burst open. The captain ordered everyone to flee into the lifeboat. They grabbed their instruments in a hurry and got away. They planned to float nearby in the water to watch and see if the ship would burst into flames, but found that they could not return the lifeboat to the fast-moving ship.

Questions:
- Was there smoke on board the *Mary Celeste?*
- What could have caused an explosion?
- Was there a hatch open on the *Mary Celeste*?
- Did the *Mary Celeste* show any evidence of a fire?

Likelihood Score:

Weather Theory

The ship suddenly encountered a very large storm that threatened to sink her. The crew became scared and got into the lifeboat in hopes of saving their lives. The lifeboat sank with the entire crew aboard.

Questions:
- What did the log book say about bad weather on the trip?
- Could Captain Briggs handle a ship like the *Mary Celeste*?
- Did the ship show any signs of a storm?

Likelihood Score:

Briggs and *Dei Gratia* Conspiracy Theories

Directions: Look at each investigation below separately. Answer the questions, refering back to the background information and your graphic organizer page for answers. Then make a judgment about the theory based on a scale of 1 to 10 with 10 being the most likely (highest) theory and 1 being the least likely (lowest) theory.

Briggs Conspiracy

Captain Briggs planned to make his crew disappear and collect the insurance money through his good friend, Captain Morehouse. They made the final plans at dinner just before the *Mary Celeste* embarked. He had his crew get into the lifeboat and sail away to the closest islands, the Azores. They would live on the island and wait for Captain Morehouse to collect the money and give half of it to them. They would live secretly on the island forever.

Questions:
- Would Captain Briggs involve his wife and child in his plan?
- What kind of person was Captain Briggs?
- Would Captain Briggs be willing to leave behind his son in New York?

Likelihood Score: ☐

Dei Gratia Conspiracy

When Captain Morehouse saw his friend's ship, he decided he wanted the ship and its cargo. He had his men attack the crew and kill all of them. Their bodies were dumped overboard and the lifeboat was released from the side of the ship. He then instructed his crew to clean up the ship and take it to Gibraltar so that they could get the money due them.

Questions:
- What kind of relationship did the two captains have with each other?
- How much money was Captain Morehouse to gain from taking over the ship?
- Did the ship show any signs of a struggle?
- Was there any evidence to prove foul play on board the ship?

Likelihood Score: ☐

The Mystery of the Mary Celeste

A New Stamp for *Mary Celeste*

Directions: Your investigative firm believes it has solved the mystery of the missing crew aboard the *Mary Celeste* Now it is time to create a commemorative stamp for the United States Post Office. Draw your new stamp that solves the mystery in the rectangle below. Be ready to present your stamp and theory to the class.

The Sinking of the Lusitania

Teacher Lesson Plan

Standard/Objective

* Develop critical sensitivities, such as empathy and skepticism, regarding attitudes, values, and behaviors of people in different historical contexts. (NCSS)

* Students will participate as passengers on the *Lusitania* in a simulation and then sit on a panel to judge the mystery of the sinking.

Materials

* Copies of the *Attention Grabber* (page 119); *Graphic Organizer* (page 120); *Background Information* (pages 124–126); *The British Planned the Sinking of the* Lusitania (page 128); *Debunking the Conspiracy Theory!* (page 129)

* Copies or overhead of the Lusitania *Course Map* (page 127)

* Overhead of the *German Warning* (page 121) and Lusitania *Simulation* (pages 122–123)

* Maps and globes

Discussion Questions

* What are some things that you will need on this trip?

* What will it be like to sail on an ocean liner?

* Are there any precautions you should take when sailing accros the ocean?

* What is going on in the world in 1915?

The Activity: Day 1

Hand the *Attention Grabber* (ticket for the trip) (page 119) to each student as he or she enters the classroom. Some students will be staying in first class accommodations and others will be in second or third class accommodations. Tell students that they should get ready because they will be embarking on their journey tomorrow. At that time, students will need to give you the ticket to board the ship. This should spark some interest in the students as they wonder where this ticket will lead them. At this point, inform students that they have traveled back in time to 1915 and are about to board a deluxe ocean liner. Since they will be onboard a ship for the next week, they are not allowed to find out any information about this journey except what is presented to them in class.

Note: The simulation will go on for a few days, and students should not be allowed to search for information outside of class.

Provide each student with a copy of the *Graphic Organizer* (page 120) for the trip. Have students write their names on these log books. Explain that on cruises, passengers recorded things in log books like this. Students might want to staple pages to the back to provide more space for writing. Tell students that these log books will serve as their graphic organizers. They are to record any information they find out about the ship and their impressions of the cruise on this paper.

The Sinking of the Lusitania

Teacher Lesson Plan *(cont.)*

The Activity: Day 1 (cont.)

Have students take out a scrap sheet of paper and make a list of what they will take on this journey. Tell students that since it is the year 1915, they can only pack things that would have existed back at that time. To make this simulation seem real, you might have students bring in a suitcase the following day packed with all the things they think they will need for the trip. The time frame of 1915 will prevent their bringing any digital or electronic devices not allowed on school premises. End the class by asking the discussion questions above. Allow students to add more items to their list during this discussion. For the last discussion question, teachers might need to allow students to look in encyclopedias to remind them that WWI was raging through Europe.

The Activity: Day 2

Place a copy of the *German Warning* (page 121) on the overhead projector for students to see when they arrive in class. Don't say anything about the advertisement. Remind students to give you their tickets.

Welcome them aboard the *Lusitania*. It might be helpful to have a sign at the door directing those boarding the *Lusitania* to enter. Acting very matter of fact, take their tickets and introduce yourself as the captain, William Turner. Wearing a nametag and a captain's hat would make a nice touch for this day. If someone asks about the advertisement on the overhead, just brush it off. Tell them that the United States is not at war with Germany and that no German in their right mind would attack a ship with women and children aboard. Even if the Germans wanted to, their submarines are no match for the fastest ocean liner called the *Lusitania*. Remind students to record any information about the *Lusitania* on the *Graphic Organizer* (page 120) that you distributed the previous day.

When everyone is settled in the classroom, announce that the *Lusitania* has left New York, is now in the Atlantic Ocean, and is heading toward its final destination, Liverpool, England. Let students look at maps and globes to see the path they will be traveling. Announce that the *Lusitania* will be traveling through the Irish Channel to get to Liverpool.

Allow a few moments for students to participate in activities that the people on the *Lusitania* might have done. For example, they can play games, walk the decks, and learn new dances. Those with first class tickets might enjoy a nice snack in the first class lounge. The second and third class passengers might receive a snack, too, but they must not enter the lounge area. Give students a few moments to write their feelings in their log books.

Finally, tell all students to close their eyes and listen to the *Lusitania Simulation* (page 122) that you will read aloud. Then provide students time to write about their experiences in their log books.

Teacher Lesson Plan *(cont.)*

The Activity: Day 3

Begin by distributing copies of the *Background Information* (page 124–126) to students. This information will be more meaningful because students have participated as passengers aboard the *Lusitania*. Distribute copies or display an overhead of the Lusitania *Course Map* (page 127) so that students have a visual of the paths that the *Lusitania* and the German submarine took.

Divide the class into two groups. Tell students that they, as former passengers on the *Lusitania*, will be participating on a committee to judge whether or not there was a British conspiracy (cover up) to sink the *Lusitania*. One group will present the evidence that supports the conspiracy and the other group will present the evidence that debunks the conspiracy. Distribute copies of *The British Planned the Sinking of the Lusitania* (page 128) and *Debunking the Conspiracy Theory* (page 129) to the appropriate groups. Instruct both groups not to share their information. Give students a few moments to think about how they will present their information to the panel on the following day. Allow students to bring in props for their presentations.

The Activity: Day 4

Let each group present their information. Begin with the group that blames the British for planning a conspiracy. Then have the group that debunks the conspiracy present last. Do not allow the committee to discuss their opinions. Tell them to think about all the evidence and claims overnight. They will have a chance to voice their opinions on the following day.

The Activity: Day 5

At the beginning of class, allow students to choose sides regarding the conspiracy. Those who support that the British planned the sinking of the *Lusitania* should group together. Those who do not believe any conspiracy took place should group together. Each group should write a statement presenting its views and the evidence that supports it. These statements can be read at the end of class. Finally, have students record their final thoughts on the mystery of the *Lusitania* in their log books.

For an added extension, students might want to research William Turner's other amazing shipwrecks. They might be interested to know that the *Lusitania* was not his first!

Attention Grabber

Directions: Copy this page and cut the tickets apart. Distribute only one ticket to each student. Some students will receive a first class ticket (they are the wealthy ones), other students will receive second or third class tickets (they are not so wealthy).

Cunard Line	**Cunard Line**	**Cunard Line**
The Finest, Fastest and Largest Steamers in the World	*The Finest, Fastest and Largest Steamers in the World*	*The Finest, Fastest and Largest Steamers in the World*

R. M. S. Lusitania	*R. M. S. Lusitania*	*R. M. S. Lusitania*
Captain William Thomas Turner	Captain William Thomas Turner	Captain William Thomas Turner
First Class Passage	**Second Class Passage**	**Third Class Passage**
Date Depart: May 1, 1915	*Date Depart:* May 1, 1915	*Date Depart:* May 1, 1915
Sails From: New York, NY	*Sails From:* New York, NY	*Sails From:* New York, NY
Your attention is specially directed to the conditions of transportation in the enclosed contract.	*Your attention is specially directed to the conditions of transportation in the enclosed contract.*	*Your attention is specially directed to the conditions of transportation in the enclosed contract.*
The company's liability for baggage is strongly limited, but passengers can protect themselves by insurance.	*The company's liability for baggage is strongly limited, but passengers can protect themselves by insurance.*	*The company's liability for baggage is strongly limited, but passengers can protect themselves by insurance.*

Graphic Organizer

Passenger's Log Book

Average Coal Consumption: about 1,000 tons a day

Name of Passenger: _____

Launched: June 7, 1906

Length: 785 feet

German Warning

NOTICE!

TRAVELLERS intending to embark on the Atlantic voyage are reminded that a state of war exists between Germany and her allies and Great Britain and her allies; that the zone of war includes the waters adjacent to the British Isles; that, in accordance with formal notice given by the Imperial German Government, vessels flying the flag of Great Britain, or any of her allies, are liable to destruction in those waters and that travellers sailing in the war zone on ships of Great Britain or her allies do so at their own risk.

IMPERIAL GERMAN EMBASSY
WASHINGTON, D. C.,   APRIL 22, 1915

ij61

Lusitania Simulation

The fresh breeze of the ocean feels wonderful as you relax on the deck of the *Lusitania*. You've been waiting for such an experience as this for your family vacation. You hate it that this trip has been spoiled by anxious thoughts. Earlier this morning you awoke to see very thick fog outside. Since then, the fog has lifted and the day is totally clear and sunny.

You find your mind wandering back to the warning in the newspaper you read the morning that you left New York. It suddenly fills you with fear, and you make yourself stop thinking about it. You get up and quickly walk into the dining lounge. You feel your stomach grumbling and decide to order some cake. Just when you get your food, you overhear other passengers talking about the stowaways that were found onboard just a few days ago. They only spoke German! Your mind wanders back to that German warning in the paper. Could these men be spies? Do they have bombs to blow up the ship? Shivers run down your spine.

As the ship begins to approach the British Isles, you and the other passengers have become uneasy. Even though you are an American, most of the passengers on this ship are British. Great Britain is in a war with Germany. You feel relieved that the U.S. is not involved in the war. The newspapers reported that German submarines lurk in the waters around the British Isles. Surely, the Germans wouldn't attack a ship with so many Americans on it. Well, at least there are enough lifeboats to take everyone to safety if something did happen.

You notice that the lifeboats have been swung over the side of the ship just this morning. They are ready to be lowered quickly if a crisis arises. You think about last night. A sailor came by your room and covered up the portholes so that your light wouldn't shine outside the ship. You went outside and noticed that all the lights were out. Not wanting to stumble around, you went back to your room. You didn't sleep much and your neck is hurting. You stop to rub it.

You finish your cake and go back outside for some air. You can see the Irish coast, and that comforts you. It's not too far away. All of a sudden, you notice the water bubbling in the distance. You see something that was longer than an automobile and round as a steering wheel. Your heart begins racing. This thing is coming at a fast speed right at the boat! Then you hear a sailor yell, "Torpedo!"

Lusitania Simulation *(cont.)*

You feel the impact. It sounds like a banging door on a windy day. Then you hear a low rumble. You know the ship has been hit. People begin pouring onto the deck screaming and running over others. Everyone is panicking. Frantically you look around for your family. You race back to the cabin and find the life jackets. Your fingers fumble as you tie one on. You grab the other jackets and run out. The minutes tick by, and the ship gets lower and lower at the front.

You rush to the back of the ship to keep from being pulled under, and it is there that you see your family waiting for you. It is impossible to get in one of the lifeboats, they are dangling too far away from the leaning ship. So, you convince your family to jump into the water. Each of them takes a jacket and puts it on as fast as they can. The time continues to tick and you know there is not much time left. You grab hands and jump together. The icy water takes your breath away. Not too far away is a boat. You yell out for help, but they say they can't help you. They are too full and can't risk tipping the boat to take on another family. What??? You are disgusted that they won't help someone in need.

You see another boat in the distance and swim over to it. Your body is aching. The water is choppy and it takes all your strength to swim. The sides of the boat are collapsed, but it has a wooden bottom. You drag your body onto the bottom and then proceed to put up the sides of the boat with the metal bars. It works, and you use all your strength to paddle back to your family. Along the way you pick up many people crying out for help. Some of these are children. Suddenly, a huge wave rocks your boat. You blink your eyes unbelievingly. The *Lusitania* is gone! You close your eyes, wishing that this were all a dream. You finally make it to a fishing boat that is taking people ashore. You fall unconscious. Your exhausted body cannot handle any more of the stress.

The Sinking of the Lusitania

Background Information

May 1, 1915, began as a rainy day. More than 1,000 passengers prepared to board the world's fastest and most beautiful ocean liner, the *Lusitania*. The *Lusitania* was an English ocean liner. Many were nervous that morning as they opened the New York paper and read a warning posted by the German embassy. But only a few canceled their plans to ride the *Lusitania* to England.

England had been in a war with Germany for more than a year at this point. The United States had remained neutral. Woodrow Wilson was the U.S. President at the time. He viewed the war as a conflict between European countries. He wanted to keep his country out of it.

Just hours before leaving, the crew was busy preparing the ship. Carriages with packages began arriving and reporters surrounded the area. The German warning made this sailing particularly newsworthy. Some even yelled out, "Take your last picture of this ocean liner! It won't be coming back!" The crew talked amongst themselves about the warning. Some even noticed that Dowie, the cat, had run away the night before. They wondered, "Could this be a bad omen?"

It was quite confusing on the ship. United States Secret Service men tried to check each bag to its owner. Private detectives looked for anyone who appeared to be a German. They wondered if the Germans planned to bring explosives aboard the ship. Rich and poor alike bustled aboard the ship. Parents struggled with their small children and their bags. The traffic jam of horse-drawn carriages on the shore was quite a sight from the ship.

A day into the trip, rumors spread aboard the ship that three stowaways were caught hiding in the steward's pantry. They only spoke German, too. Were they spies? Passengers suddenly remembered the warning in the paper. To keep them from doing any harm, these three men were kept locked away the rest of the trip.

A day before the *Lusitania* set sail, a German submarine left her base in Germany. This was the newest of the small submarines that could carry up to seven torpedoes and travel 5,000 miles. The captain knew he had to be extra careful to bypass the British warships. These warships could easily cut a submarine in half. The captain was also aware that nets were hung around the harbors in England. These nets were used for catching submarines and many of them had bombs called *mines*. The submarine headed for the waters around Liverpool. The orders were to strike any ship carrying soldiers to Europe. The captain knew that the *Lusitania* was headed his way. He could only hope to encounter this ocean liner in the vast ocean water.

The Sinking of the Lusitania

Background Information (cont.)

The submarine had good luck. They managed to sink a small British schooner and two British steamer ships in just two days. Instead of heading toward Liverpool, the captain chose to wait in the Irish Channel. He reasoned that it would take up too much fuel to go there. Maybe he would encounter some other ships in this channel to sink before heading back to Germany.

Passengers aboard this ocean liner had amused themselves by playing shuffleboard, dealing cards, and dancing the latest dances like the Turkey Trot and the Bunny Hug. Some were bored and longed for a little excitement.

The *Lusitania* was equipped with 22 wooden lifeboats. It also had 26 boats with wooden bottoms and collapsible sides that were easier to store onboard. There was room in these for everyone aboard if the boat did sink. Each cabin had enough life jackets, too. But few took the time to examine how to get them on properly.

Captain Turner did not think it was necessary to order that passengers take part in evacuation drills. He believed it would only upset the passengers. He also firmly believed that no submarine could catch a boat that went as fast as the *Lusitania*. However, on this trip, the *Lusitania* was not going at full speed. One boiler room was shut down to conserve coal. Even with the ship running a little slower, the captain was still convinced that a submarine could not catch her. Furthermore, torpedoes were not that accurate. The chances of being hit, according to Turner, were very slim.

Just two days before the scheduled landing in Liverpool, Captain Turner was handed a message from the British Navy. It said, "Submarines active off south coast of Ireland." He was not told that 26 ships were sunk in these very waters during the six days the *Lusitania* had been at sea. Turner began taking some precautions. He had the lifeboats ready to be lowered. All the outside lights were put out and any cabin skylights or portholes were covered up. This would make the ship almost invisible at night. Sailors stood on the decks as lookouts for any submarines.

That night, Turner made an announcement to the passengers. He told them of the danger ahead, but reassured them that they would be safe in the hands of the Royal Navy. The passengers worried. Some even chose to sleep in the lounge areas instead of in their cabins. Getting to the deck from the lounge was much easier if something were to happen.

The Sinking of the Lusitania

Background Information (cont.)

The next day, Friday, May 7, the *Lusitania* entered the Irish Channel. It was a very foggy morning, so the *Lusitania* was going unusually slow. Even when the fog lifted, the ship still seemed to be sluggish. For some unknown reason, the naval escort ship withdrew from the *Lusitania*. The German submarine surfaced that afternoon to see it in the distance. The captain could hardly believe his eyes! He ordered his submarine to dive down 35 feet. Then the submarine tried to catch the huge ocean liner. He noticed the ship changing her course, and then changing it again. Suddenly, the ship began coming directly toward his submarine. He exclaimed, "She could not be steering a more perfect course if she was deliberately trying to give us a dead shot!" He ordered his men to fire the torpedo. He chose to ignore the international law that said he must first give them warning before firing. He did not allow any time for the passengers to get off the ship before the torpedo hit.

The *Lusitania* had been in route for six days from the harbor of New York to a destination it never saw: Liverpool, England. When the *Lusitania* was hit, the hull exploded like a bomb in a tunnel. The ocean liner threw people about as it began to sink into the Atlantic. As the ship tilted to the front and the right, people panicked, and the few who could find lifeboats survived. Others jumped into the sea as the groaning and moaning of the drowning ship deafened their screams. The liner balanced for a moment straight up on its bow, which had struck the ocean floor, before it disappeared from sight. It took only 18 minutes after firing the torpedo for the 785-foot ship to sink. Public officials could not believe that Germany would attack a civilian-filled ocean liner with women and children aboard, as well as many Americans. A total of 1,201 men, women, and children lost their lives, including 128 Americans. *Lusitania's* captain, William Turner, survived the wreck by holding onto a piece of the ship's wreckage. He washed up on the shore after being in the icy water for three hours.

Lusitania Course Map

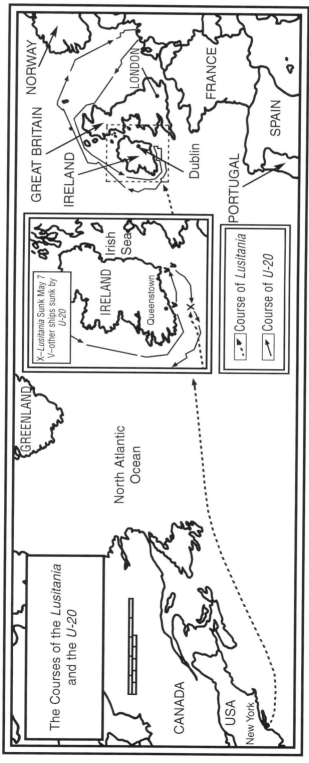

The British Planned the Sinking of the *Lusitania*

Directions: You are a witness who will testify before the committee of surviving passengers. Each person in your group will choose one of the statements below to present to the class. You must think of a creative way to present this information in your own words.

- The British government wanted the U.S. to enter the war to help the Allies. Even a U.S. congressman named Richmond Hobson believed that the British had the entire sinking arranged to bring the United States into the war.

- The Admiralty gave Turner orders to zigzag the ship and to sail at full speed in the middle of the harbor. Captain Turner did not obey these orders. He slowed down as he approached the channel, sailed too close to the shore where submarines were known to lurk, and during the six-day cruise he did not order any evacuation drills to prepare his crew.

- The German Kaiser told the United States ambassador that he believed the British "made the *Lusitania* go slowly in English waters so that the Germans could torpedo it and so bring on trouble."

- Instead of slowing down, Turner could have gotten to Liverpool at high tide by zigzagging at 21 knots, the full speed of the ship.

- At the time of the torpedo, the ships portholes were open and thus enabled the ship to flood quickly and sink.

- Turner admitted that his crew was well below peacetime standards. In other words, they were not prepared for any emergency. He did nothing to prepare his crew for an emergency.

- Three days before the disaster, several passengers asked Turner to conduct emergency boat drills. He did not conduct one drill.

- For some unknown reason, the British naval escort ship withdrew from the *Lusitania*, leaving it vulnerable in a submarine-filled channel.

The Sinking of the Lusitania

Debunking the Conspiracy Theory!

You are a witness who will testify before the committee of surviving passengers. Each person in your group will choose one of the statements below to present to the class. You must think of a creative way to present this information in your own words.

- Germany did not want the U.S. to enter the war, therefore, warnings were posted in the paper.

- Although this was not confirmed, the *Lusitania* was believed to have carried munitions on board to supply the British. Germany had a right to fire at any vessel carrying munitions.

- Turner says that he delayed the speed so that the ship would arrive in Liverpool on high tide rather than hang around dangerous submarine hunting ground.

- The British Navy used Turner as a scapegoat after the *Lusitania* disaster. They claimed that he was not competent to handle a boat like the *Lusitania*. He was sent to trial.

- Torpedoes at this time were highly likely to go astray. Technology was not able to prevent a misfire either. Big ships like the *Lusitania* could survive even a direct hit by a torpedo and make their way to a port nearby.

- The odds of a ship going down just after one hit by a torpedo were extremely small.

- The British were buying munitions from the U.S. If the United States were to have entered the war at that time, the munitions would no longer be available for the British to buy. The United States would need all of its munitions to support its own army. The British knew this, and they desperately needed the munitions. They did not want the U.S. to enter the war at that time.

- The Royal Navy did not have enough escort vessels for all their ships. They did not want the Germans to know about that shortage for fear that the Germans would send more submarines to the area.

- Recent excavations of the ship prove that the ship went down so quickly because the torpedo hit the area where the coal fueled the ship. That hit caused a huge explosion in the front of the ship, leaving a large hole which water began to fill.

The Missing Bones of Peking Man

Teacher Lesson Plan

Standard/Objective

❋ Demonstrate an understanding that different scholars may describe the same event or situation in different ways but must provide reasons or evidence for their views. (NCSS)

❋ Acting as archaeologists, students will solve the mystery of the missing Peking Man bones, create broadcasts to announce the news, and plan an excavation of the site where the bones lay.

Materials

❋ copies of the *Graphic Organizer* (page 134); *Background Information* (pages 135–137); *Peking Man Map* (page 138); *The William Foley Account* (page 139); *Other Marine Accounts* (page 140); *The Japanese Took the Bones* (page 141) *Advertising for the Bones* (page 142); *Planning an Expedition* (page 143)

❋ an overhead copy of the *Attention Grabber* (page 133)

❋ shoeboxes

❋ dirt

❋ toothbrushes

❋ colored pencils

Discussion Questions

❋ What do you think this is?

❋ Who did this belong to?

❋ What is so mysterious about this skull?

❋ Look closely. Point out any distinguishing features on this skull.

❋ Do you think this is a skull from a person or an animal? Why?

The Activity: Day 1

If possible, begin this mystery with a small archaeological dig in the classroom. Have students bring in shoeboxes and an old toothbrush. Have students gather some dirt or sand from outside to place inside the boxes until the boxes are at least half full. Have them hide at least five things from their desks underneath the dirt in the shoeboxes. They should then trade boxes with friends, using their toothbrushes to carefully uncover the hidden artifacts. Each artifact should be recorded on paper.

Teacher Lesson Plan *(cont.)*

The Activity: Day 1 (cont.)

When students have finished their excavations, place an overhead of the *Attention Grabber* (page 133) on the overhead projector. Tell students to imagine that they uncovered this in their boxes. Ask the discussion questions above. Distribute copies of the *Graphic Organizer* (page 134) and explain that students will keep the information that they learn about this skull and the mystery on this page.

Then distribute copies of the *Background Information* (pages 135–137) and read it aloud as a class. Stop and clarify information if students have questions. Give students time to write down any information that they might feel is important on their graphic organizers. Tell them to keep their graphic organizers handy to write more information about this mystery for the remainder of the week.

The Activity: Day 2

Distribute copies of the *Peking Man Map* (page 138) to show students the planned route of the bones. Have students look at the *Background Information* again. Using colored pencils or crayons, tell students to work with partners to map out several of the theories. For example, students can draw a route showing that the bones went to Japan.

Then distribute copies of *The William Foley Account* (page 139). This is the first of four theories that explain what happened to the bones. Read this aloud as a class. Ask students the following questions:

- What seems to be believable about William Foley's story?

- What causes you to question his story?

Let students record important information about this theory on their graphic organizers. Allow students to form small groups (three or four to a group). Then have them create broadcasts about this theory. The broadcasts can be formatted to either radio or television. The broadcasts should be presented in a way that claims to solve the mystery about the Peking Man bones. Students can embellish the facts to make their point. Allow groups to present their broadcasts to the class.

The Activity: Day 3

Remind students about the information discussed the previous day regarding William Foley. Then distribute copies of *Other Marine Accounts* (page 140). Read this theory aloud as a class and ask students the following questions:

- What seems to be believable about these marine accounts?

- What causes you to question this story?

Let students record important information about this theory on their graphic organizer. Allow students to form small groups (three or four to a group). Like the day before, have groups create broadcasts about this theory. The broadcasts can be formatted to either radio or television. Allow groups to present their broadcasts to the class.

The Missing Bones of Peking Man

Teacher Lesson Plan *(cont.)*

The Activity: Day 4

Refresh students' memories about the two theories regarding William Foley and the other marines. Then distribute copies of *The Japanese Took the Bones* (page 141). Read this theory together as a class. This theory could have three different scenarios. Ask students the following questions:

- Of all three of these scenarios, which seems to be more believable?
- What story seems to be least likely and why?

Let students record important information about this theory on their graphic organizers. Allow students to form small groups (three or four to a group). As the day before, have groups create a broadcast about this theory. The broadcasts can be formatted to either radio or television. Allow groups to present their broadcasts to the class.

The Activity: Day 5

Begin by refreshing students' memories about the three theories they have read about. Then distribute copies of *Advertising for the Bones* (page 142). This theory will perhaps be the most intriguing of all the theories. Read the information together as a class and ask the following questions.

- What seems to be believable about Christopher Janus' story?
- What causes them to question this story?

Let students record important information about this theory on their graphic organizers. Allow students to form small groups (three or four to a group). As the day before, have groups create broadcasts about this theory. The broadcast can be formatted to either radio or television. Allow groups to present their broadcasts to the class.

Then distribute copies of *Planning an Expedition* (page 143). At this point, students have had time to think about many of the theories. They will use this sheet to show their final decisions about what happened to the bones. If time permits, allow students to share their opinions with the class or post these opinions on a bulletin board so that others can read the differing opinions.

Attention Grabber

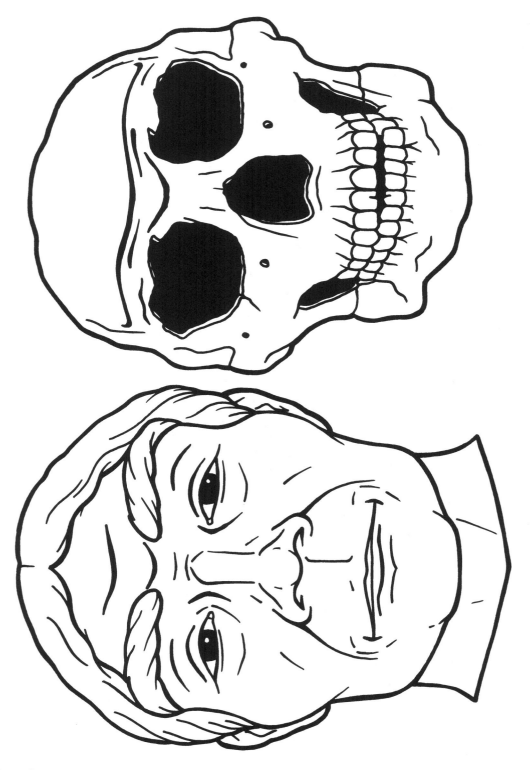

Graphic Organizer

Digging Up Evidence

Directions: Record information on this page about the mystery of the missing Peking Man bones.

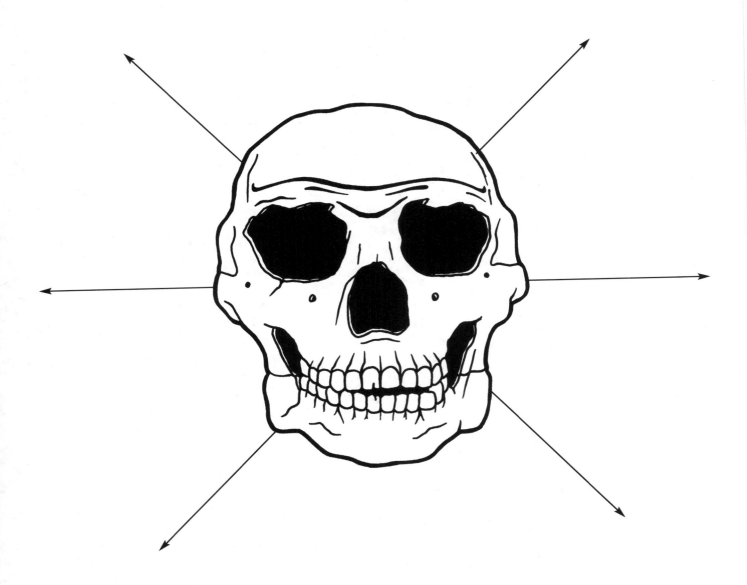

The Missing Bones of Peking Man

Background Information

Many years ago, peasants in China dug up old bones in quarries and mines and sold them to Chinese pharmacies. They believed these bones were from ancient dragons and had the power to heal sickness. In truth, these bones belonged to extinct animals that lived thousands of years ago. The pharmacies ground these bones into dust and sold them to cure almost everything from demonic possession to epilepsy. If people needed a cure, they would mix the powder with a liquid and drink it.

Archaeologists began traveling to Peking, now called Beijing, China, in hopes of finding old bones from the ancestors of man. In the early 1920s, a set of bones was found and examined by leading scientists. They believed they had found a fossil collection that included teeth from a human-like creature. These teeth were two million years old. It was the oldest evidence of man's existence ever found. For the next 14 years, archaeologists dug up many bones in that area in hopes of finding more.

In November of 1928, fragments of a skull, lower jaw, and teeth were found. With these pieces of evidence, scientists could better picture what this human-like creature looked like. This human-like creature was called Peking Man, named for the place where he was found. The site even showed that this Peking Man used fire. Over the next few years, 40 distinct sets of bones were found. Each set belonged to a different Peking man. They were more than 500,000 years old. With these bones, scientists were able to figure out what this Peking Man looked like. He was between 4 feet 8 inches and 5 feet 1 inch. He weighed 100 pounds, had a powerful body, and walked upright. His face was wide and his skull formed a large ridge over his eyes. He looked more like a human than an ape.

The archaeologists' excavation work ended quickly when the Japanese invaded China in 1937. Instead of digging, the scientists remained in the laboratory examining the bones. The laboratory was officially under the control of the United States, and since Japan was not at war with the U.S., they left the lab alone (until after the bombing of Pearl Harbor). The Japanese held the city of Peking for four long years. In 1941, one of the scientists, Franz Weidenreich, thought the bones were in danger of being taken or destroyed by the Japanese. He wanted the bones to be moved to the United States for safekeeping. The other scientists refused his idea, so he made plaster casts of the bones and took the casts with him. These casts still exist today.

Background Information *(cont.)*

By the fall, the other scientists changed their minds. The bones would be sent to the American Museum of Natural History until it was safe to return to China. They decided to secretly ship the bones to the United States through the Marine Corps. The scientists carefully packed the bones into two large wooden crates. These crates were stored for about two days at the laboratory, and then they were transferred to the U.S. offices next door to the Marine Corps. There is no record of the crates' delivery at the Marine barracks, but the scientists believe they made it there.

The plan was for the Marines to take the bones and place them on the *U.S.S. President Harrison*. This boat was scheduled to leave the port on December 8th. Unfortunately, war broke out between the U.S. and Japan with the bombing of Pearl Harbor on December 7th. It is known that the bones never made it to the *U.S.S. President Harrison*. The Japanese sunk the boat before it reached the port where it was to pick up the bones. Somewhere along the way, the bones disappeared without a trace.

On December 8th, the Japanese stormed the laboratory looking for the bones. They knew these bones were valuable and had been snooping around the excavation site. They looked in the United States Embassy and at the Marine barracks, but nothing could be found.

Throughout the last 50 years, many have had theories about where these bones ended up. One theory is that a few Marines were assigned to guard the crates. They took the crates on a train, but the train was stormed by Japanese soldiers. These soldiers threw out the luggage and it is believed the bones were lost and destroyed in the process. In a deathbed confession, a Japanese soldier claimed that he buried the bones under an ancient tree in Peking. The tree was found, but not the bones.

The Missing Bones of Peking Man

Background Information *(cont.)*

In 1945, two Marines claimed that they were in charge of the bones. They dropped the bones at a warehouse at the port and never saw the bones again. Some believe the fossils were buried at the Marine compound in China in hopes of being dug up after the war. A U.S. Navy lieutenant said he had possession of the bones in China. He claimed that he gave the bones to some friends of his for safekeeping. Those friends have never been identified.

In the mid 1970s, a Chicago businessman named Christopher Janus placed an advertisement in the newspaper. He offered a reward to any information leading to the discovery of the bones. One woman contacted him and said she had the bones. She arranged a secret meeting and gave a picture of the bones as proof that she had them. After the newspapers found out about the story, she never contacted Janus again.

Still some think that the bones were smuggled out of Peking and are in the United States. Were these bones destroyed? Does someone have them hidden in secret? Or are they still in China? Until they are found, the Peking Man bones will remain a mystery.

The Missing Bones of Peking Man

Peking Man Map

Directions: This map shows the expected route of the Peking Man bones from China to the United States.

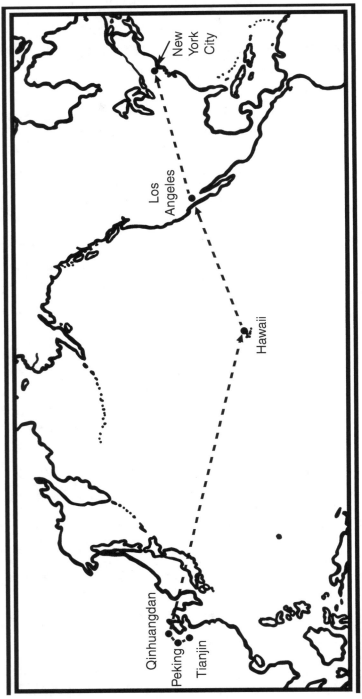

The William Foley Account

William Foley surfaced in the 1970s with his story that he was the person entrusted with the crates of bones. He was a U.S. Navy lieutenant. He took the crates to the port of Qinhuangdao just east of Peking (Beijing). When Pearl Harbor was bombed, all U.S. soldiers in China were taken as prisoners of war. Since Foley was an officer, he was given a few days before he had to report to prison camp. He said that during those days he left the crates with two Chinese friends who lived in Tianjin. He never gave the names of his Chinese friends.

In 1980, relations between China and the U.S. had improved. A scientist who was part of the excavation in the 1930s wrote to Foley asking him to return. This scientist wanted help finding the bones. Foley agreed to come only if he could meet with important officials in the Chinese government. The trip never happened, and he died in 1992.

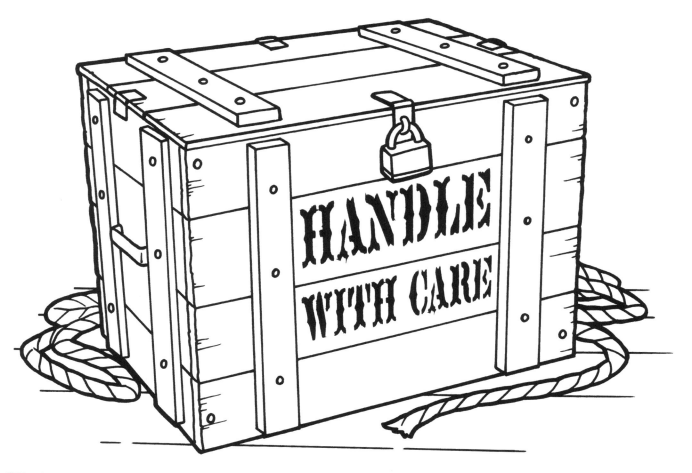

Other Marine Accounts

An interview conducted in 1945 of two Marines was recently found. These two marines said that they delivered the crates to a Swiss warehouse at the Chinese port where the crates should have been loaded on the *U.S.S. President Harrison*. The crates remained there in hopes of being shipped to the U.S. However, there is no other evidence to support this claim. No records show that the crates arrived at the Swiss warehouse, but the operation of moving the bones was to be kept a secret. It is conceivable that the records in that warehouse would not show the arrival of the bones.

The Japanese Took the Bones

The Japanese seized the bones from the Marines when they were taken to prison camp. Three things could have happened to the bones from that point.

1. The bones were put aboard the Japanese fishing boat called the *Awa Maru*. In April of 1945, an American submarine torpedoed the boat. The bones went down with the boat. The Chinese tried to salvage the wreck at the bottom of the ocean in 1977, but had no luck.

2. The Japanese secretly hid the bones somewhere in Japan. Even though U.S. troops searched Japan for the bones after the war, they could not find the hiding place.

3. A Japanese soldier made a confession on his deathbed in 1966. He claimed that the Japanese government seized the Peking Man bones and entrusted them to his care. When the Japanese were defeated in 1945, he was ordered to bury the bones under an ancient pine tree. He made a specific mark on the tree. When the Chinese heard this story, they found the marked tree, but could not find any bones. They believed the Japanese dug up the bones and took them.

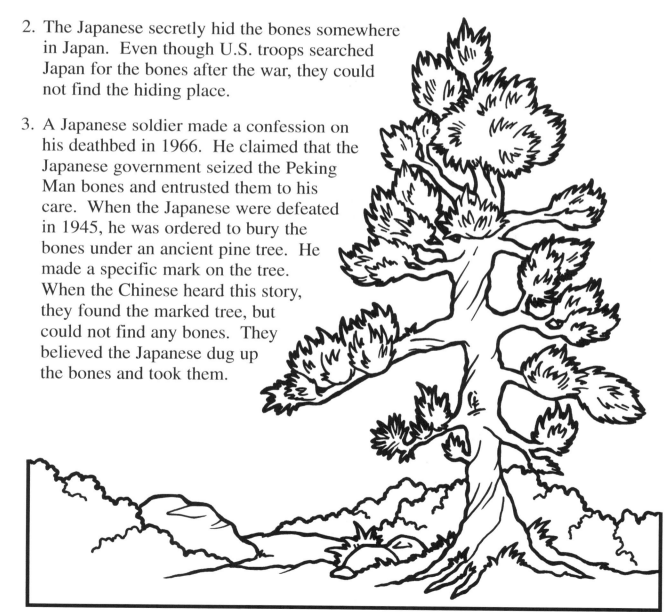

Advertising for the Bones

In the mid 1970s, a Chicago businessman named Christopher Janus decided to solve this mystery once and for all. He had just returned from a trip to China. The Chinese had asked him to help them locate the missing bones. When he returned to the U.S., he advertised an award of $5,000 to anyone who could produce the bones of Peking Man. He received hundreds of letters from people who did not know the least thing about the bones. But he did receive one very important phone call from a mysterious woman who claimed she had the bones. Her voice sounded very nervous. She refused to give her name but agreed to meet with him at the top of the Empire State Building in New York City.

Janus said the woman was in her late 40s. She claimed that her deceased husband was a U.S. Marine during World War II. He was stationed in China during that time. When he came back from the war, he brought a box full of bones with him. He believed these fossils were the Peking Man bones and told his wife to keep this secret. Her husband had recently died and she needed the money. She gave Janus a photo of the bones and demanded $500,000. Janus gave the photo to a very experienced scientist to see if these were the real bones. He compared the casts with the photo and found one skull that looked to be authentic. Other scientists agreed, but the photo was not very clear, so nothing could be known for certain unless the bones could be examined. The press made a big deal of this during the time, and the woman became scared. She never contacted Janus again. Janus wrote a book about the experience.

The Missing Bones of Peking Man

Planning an Expedition

Directions: You have solved the mystery of the missing Peking Man bones and you know where these bones are located. On this page draw the excavation site where the bones are hidden and explain how you came to your conclusion.

Excavation Site:

How I came to this conclusion:

Bibliography

Books

Altman, Gail S. *Beethoven: A Man of His Words.*

Ballard, Robert D. *Exploring the Lusitania: Probing the Mysteries of the Sinking that Changed History.*

Cohen, Daniel. *Missing! Stories of Strange Disappearances.*

Preston, Diana. *Remember the Lusitania!*

Simon, Seymour. *Strange Mysteries from Around the World.*

Stewart, Robert. *Mysteries of History.*

Yolen, Jane. *The Mary Celeste: An Unsolved Mystery from History.*

Websites

The Oak Island Treasure
http://www.oakislandtreasure.co.uk/index.html

The Marco Polo Odyssey with National Geographic
http://magma.nationalgeographic.com/ngm/data/2001/07/01/sights_n_sounds/media.2.2.html

The Man in the Iron Mask
http://www.royalty.nu/legends/IronMask.html

The Mystery of the Mary Celeste
http://www.mysteriesofcanada.com/Nova_Scotia/mary_celeste.htm

Peking Man Reconstruction
http://www.modernhumanorigins.com/pekingman1.html

The Shakespeare Authorship
www.shakespeareauthorship.com

The Marlow Society
www.marlowe-society.org/

The Shakespeare Question
www.princeton.edu/~rbivens/shakespeare/

Beethoven's Immortal Beloved
www.lvbeethoven.com/Amours/ImmortalAbout.html
www.usnews.com/usnews/doubleissue/mysteries/immortal.htm

Mysteries and Secrets–Mozart
www.skygaze.com/content/mysteries/Mozart.shtml